## JACK THORNE

Jack Thorne's plays for the stage include *Harry Potter and the Cursed Child* (Palace Theatre, London, 2016); *The Solid Life of Sugar Water* (Graeae Theatre Company); *Hope* (Royal Court Theatre, London, 2014); adaptations of *Let the Right One In* (National Theatre of Scotland at Dundee Rep, the Royal Court and the Apollo Theatre, London, 2013/14) and *Stuart: A Life Backwards* (Underbelly, Edinburgh, and tour, 2013); *Mydidae* (Soho, 2012; Trafalgar Studios, 2013); an adaptation of Friedrich Dürrenmatt's *The Physicists* (Donmar Warehouse, 2012); *Bunny* (Underbelly, Edinburgh, 2010; Soho, 2011); *2nd May 1997* (Bush, 2009); *Burying Your Brother in the Pavement* (National Theatre Connections, 2008); *When You Cure Me* (Bush, 2005; Radio 3's Drama on Three, 2006); *Fanny and Faggot* (Pleasance, Edinburgh, 2004 and 2007; Finborough, 2007; English Theatre of Bruges, 2007; Trafalgar Studios, 2007); and *Stacy* (Tron, 2006; Arcola, 2007; Trafalgar Studios, 2007). His radio plays include *Left at the Angel* (Radio 4, 2007), an adaptation of *The Hunchback of Notre Dame* (2009) and an original play *People Snogging in Public Places* (Radio 3's Wire slot, 2009). He was a core writer in all three series of *Skins* (E4, Channel 4, BBC America), writing five episodes. His other TV writing includes *National Treasure*, *The Last Panthers*, *Glue*, *The Fades* (2012 BAFTA for Best Drama Series), *Shameless*, *Cast-Offs*, *This is England '86* (2011 Royal Television Society Award for Best Writer – Drama), *This is England '88*, *This is England '90* and the thirty-minute drama *The Spastic King*. His work for film includes the features *War Book, A Long Way Down*, adapted from Nick Hornby's novel, and *The Scouting Book for Boys*, which won him the Star of London Best Newcomer Award at the London Film Festival 2009.

Jack Thorne

# JUNKYARD

NICK HERN BOOKS
London
www.nickhernbooks.co.uk

**A Nick Hern Book**

*Junkyard* first published as a paperback original in Great Britain in 2017 by Nick Hern Books Limited, The Glasshouse, 49a Goldhawk Road, London W12 8QP

*Junkyard* copyright © 2017 Jack Thorne
Introduction copyright © 2017 Jack Thorne/Guardian News and Media

Jack Thorne has asserted his right to be identified as the author of this work

Cover image: Feast Creative

Designed and typeset by Nick Hern Books, London
Printed in the UK by Mimeo Ltd, Huntingdon, Cambridgeshire PE29 6XX

A CIP catalogue record for this book is available from the British Library

ISBN  978 1 84842 664 1

**Woodland**
**CARBON**
www.woodlandcarbon.co.uk
NICK HERN BOOKS
Printed on Carbon Captured paper

*For Mick (Mike), a boy from Walthamstow,
a playground attendant, a planner, and my Dad.*

## Introduction
*Jack Thorne*

My dad recently retired after fifty years of public service. In that time, he wore many hats: treasurer of this, secretary of that, chairman of this, agitator of that. He was a town planner, teacher, playgroup leader and union organiser. He worked in council offices, community centres, Citizens Advice Bureaus and, most recently, on a roundabout renovation.

One thing was a constant: he always worked for the public good. We grew up without much money but were never short when it came to having things of importance thrust into our heads. We went on marches, protests and holidays to union conferences in Blackpool and Bournemouth. He always expected big things of us and was never shy of saying so.

Having recently become a father, I've found myself thinking about my dad, and about how the choices I've made don't measure up to his contributions to the world. But I've also found myself thinking about the weird bits, chief among them the junk playground he built with some kids at Lockleaze School in Bristol. We used visit it regularly, particularly on Fireworks Night, when we'd sit on flimsy flammable structures while playing with fire, or go off eating hot dogs. I didn't really see the point of it. I always saw him as serious man and a playground just seemed so silly. But the more I investigated, the more appealing the slightly pirate world of these adventure playgrounds seemed.

They were set up by a woman called Lady Allen. 'There is no asphalt,' she once said, explaining their difference, 'no seesaws, swings or slides, except those created by the children themselves out of waste material freely available on the site – or by the terrain of the playground itself.' These outreach schemes were meant to encourage creativity and inventiveness, and to give children a taste of manual labour.

There are still quite a few dotted about. A mass of broken wood, disused car tyres and concrete tubes, they usually involve sheer drops, death-defying rope swings, and look like they've been set on fire a couple of times (they generally have). They're always built and designed by the kids themselves, and they change every year or so, to reflect the current intake. In a world of health and safety, they are a haven of anarchy.

In *Junkyard*, the kids are led by a man called Rick from Walthamstow. Back then, my dad was Mick from Walthamstow (although he now goes by Mike). But *Junkyard* is not about my dad. Despite him thinking he features punishingly in everything I write, I lack both the tools and the inclination to write a theatrical biography.

Rather, it's an attempt to walk the high wire he walked – and to tell the truth about the type of kids who built these playgrounds, the places they come from, the lives they lead. These are the kids no one else wants – who'll attack you, abuse you, accuse you and make you feel like shit, because no one in authority has ever reached them. It's those kids and that relationship I wanted to capture.

Because of that, right from the start, the director Jeremy Herrin and I were adamant than it shouldn't be a Mr Chips-style story, where a knight comes in and makes everyone's lives better. That's not how these things work: with kids like these, there's a constant threat of darkness just around the corner. I have worked in outreach as well (far less successfully than my dad) and know that it's about failure as much as it's about success.

It was for that reason we decided to write it as a musical, my first. They're odd beasts, musicals, but what I like about them is the way they allow windows into people. When people sing, you get an opportunity to see a vulnerability, a glimpse of a life in a messed-up head.

But *Junkyard* isn't Andrew Lloyd Webber. The music Stephen Warbeck has written is all about the kids and the playground. He's built instruments out of junk that our musicians and kids play. They frequently play the set too. Actually, by the time the show opens, I'm pretty sure they'll be banging each other's heads together for a tune – because every day the cast seems to get just a little bit wilder. Yesterday, they were kicking balls at each other's heads through The Death Hole (don't ask).

My dad once took a bunch of kids he'd been working with on a camping trip. While driving them home in the minibus, they were making a racket and he said if they didn't shut up he'd throw them out and they could walk. A pretty standard threat. But then they didn't shut up – and he was good to his word and left them on an A-road thirty miles north of Bristol. He thought he could circle back pretty quickly, but there wasn't a roundabout for miles. By the time he returned, they'd hitched. On Monday, aside from a bollocking from the headmistress, the kids all went back to work on the playground.

These junkyard playgrounds are now under the threat. The wilful destruction of local government services by George Osborne and co has left a skeleton of youth/outreach schemes. And this is the other reason I wanted to write the musical. Because, when it comes to cuts, who'd keep open a playground over a Sure Start Centre? The playgrounds, which have been burnt down so many times, are probably now under their greatest threat. But these places do capture kids that can't be captured elsewhere.

A young lad was recently killed near where I lived and I talked to his uncle about what had happened. He said quite simply there's nowhere else for these kids to go – nothing else for them to do. And if we don't reach them as kids, when else do we reach them?

It does make me proud that the playground my dad built still stands. The school it was attached to was demolished in 2009 but 'The Vench' playground lives on. One of my dad's big worries about *Junkyard* is that I'll give him too much credit: he was part of a team full of passionate people, who worked incredibly hard to make it happen. But I still consider it his playground and, when I go back there and see kids playing on it forty years on, it gives me great joy. When he's old enough to hold a hammer, I want my kid to play at The Vench, to help rebuild it and renew it. I hope the musical captures some of its indomitable spirit.

This piece was originally written for the *Guardian* in 2017 and reproduced with permission.

*Junkyard* was first performed at Bristol Old Vic Theatre on 2 March 2017 (previews from 24 February), in a co-production between Headlong, Bristol Old Vic, Rose Theatre Kingston and Theatr Clwyd. The cast was as follows:

| | |
|---|---|
| DEBBIE | Scarlett Brookes |
| RICK | Calum Callaghan |
| GINGER | Josef Davies |
| FIZ | Erin Doherty |
| MALCOLM | Kevin McMonagle |
| TALC | Enyi Okoronkwo |
| TILLY | Seyi Omooba |
| MUM | Lisa Palfrey |
| HIGGY | Jack Riddiford |
| LOPPY | Ciaran Alexander Stewart |

MUSICIANS
*Show MD and Bass*   Akintayo Akinbode
*Drums*   Nadine Lee
*Guitar*   Dario Rossetti-Bonell

*Director*   Jeremy Herrin
*Composer*   Stephen Warbeck
*Designer*   Chiara Stephenson
*Lighting Designer*   Jack Knowles
*Sound Designer*   Ian Dickinson
    for Autograph
*Musical Director*   Akintayo Akinbode
*Movement Director*   Polly Bennett
*Casting Director*   Lotte Hines CDG
*Assistant Director*   Michal Keyamo
*Costume Supervisor*   Ed Parry
*Associate Costume Supervisor*   Annelies Henny
*Music Preparation*   Andrew Green

*Production Manager*   Simon Evans
*Company Stage Manager*   Linsey Hall
*Deputy Stage Manager*   Jen Llewellyn
*Assistant Stage Manager*   Katie Barrett

# JUNKYARD

*A Play about Junk.*
*Featuring Junk Music played by a Junk Orchestra.*

The following is based on a true story.

Ish.

## Characters

KIDS
FIZ, *female*
TALC, *male*
GINGER, *male*
HIGGY, *male*
LOPPY, *male*
TILLY, *female*
DEBBIE, *female*

ADULTS
MUM
RICK
MALCOLM

## Location

A junk playground in Lockleaze. Bristol. 1979.

In the first half the playground goes up.

In the second half the playground comes down.

Ish.

*This text went to press before the end of rehearsals and so may differ slightly from the play as performed.*

## ACT ONE

### Scene One

*The stage is in total darkness.*

*Suddenly a torch runs on to the stage. Or a person holding a torch.*

*Then the torch goes out.*

GINGER      Shit.

*The torch is hit once, twice, three times, it briefly glows into light and then dies again.*

Shit.
Fucking.
This is the sort of shit that...

*A lighter is lit. A cigarette is lit. The cigarette is smoked.*

*The torch is hit again. It works suddenly.*

*It's pointed in four directions.*

Wherever you are. Wherever you are.

*Then it alights on something.*

TALC      Ginger...

GINGER      Oh shit. Oh shit.

*The torch dies again.*

TALC      I... I...

GINGER      Guys! Guys! Oh shit. Oh shit.

*He runs, he trips, he falls, he hits at the torch. It's not giving off anything now.*

Guys. Guys! GUYS!

*The lighter is relit, to pick out a prone body,
a tearful* TALC *beside it.*

TALC        Shit.

GINGER      Oh shit. Oh shit.

*The lighter goes out.*

*Then a lighter is lit elsewhere in the theatre.*

*Then another one.*

*Then another.*

*Suddenly there are eight lighters lit.*

*And then a hum starts.*

TILLY       (*Singing.*) There is a blackbird
            Sitting
            On a black post
            In the dark.
            You may not see it.
            But it's there.

            Night.
            It's the best time of the day.
            It's black. It's dark. It's secret.

            Courage sits waiting
            In a cave.
            It's got no friends.
            And it's starving
            It just waits
            And wants –

## Scene Two

*The lighters go out and the lights come up. Bang. In an instant.*
*It's magic.*

RICK *is standing alone on stage. He's hammering two large*
*pieces of wood together. He has a cigarette poking out of his lip*
*in a direction he thinks is rakish.*

FIZ *and* TALC *walk on to the stage. They're carrying a plank*
*of wood on each shoulder.* FIZ *is dressed carefully in a unisex*
*outfit. She looks well washed and cared for.* TALC *looks like he*
*hasn't seen a bath. Ever. And his clothes have never been*
*washed. He has quite a prominent milk moustache. His*
*shoelaces are untied. And broken.*

FIZ         …and she said in that case I'll keep it in a cage.
            And Mum says you're not keeping a rat in a cage.
            And she says but I like them, they're furry and
            cuddly and Mum says rats are dirty and
            dangerous. And she says dirty, dangerous, furry
            and cuddly. And Mum says dirty and dangerous
            are worse than –

TALC        I love your mum.

FIZ         You love anyone will give you a feed… Anyway,
            weren't three days that my sister comes to me,
            'think it might be dead'. I said, 'what's dead?'
            And she said 'my rat'.

TALC        She kept the rat? I knew she would.

            *They put down the wood.* RICK *looks up at them.*
            *They turn and walk away again.*

FIZ         In Tupperware. She'd picked out a rat. Put it in
            her airtight box. To keep it safe. She were quite
            shock-ed when the fuckee expi-red.

TALC        That is nasty.

FIZ         That's not the nasty thing – the nasty thing is that
            she kept the corpse. Turned green now. She don't
            get it and stroke it no more but… I bet it's still in
            the box. Under her bed.

TALC          Your sister is…

              *They've gone. RICK looks after them. Then
              continues hammering.*

              *A girl – DEBBIE – walks on to the stage.*

DEBBIE        (*Singing.*) Don't even start.
              Don't even start.
              Don't even start to start.
              What you're starting.

              *She looks at RICK. Who concentrates on
              hammering. She exits.*

              *A guy – HIGGY – runs onstage behind her.*

HIGGY         No… No… No…

RICK          You here to help?

              *HIGGY looks up at RICK. Who is now looking
              at him.*

HIGGY         No.

RICK          We've got a lot to do.

HIGGY         Yeah. I can see.

RICK          But you don't want to help?

HIGGY         Fuck no. You seen Debbie?

RICK          Which one is Debbie?

HIGGY         Debbie. You know her.
              (*Singing.*) Dirty Debbie.
              She's always ready.

RICK          No. I haven't seen Debbie. And you probably
              shouldn't call her Dirty.

              *HIGGY looks at him, slightly disbelievingly.*

HIGGY         Debbie? Debbie?

              *RICK looks after him, smiles, pulls off his top
              and then, bare-backed, continues to hammer.*

FIZ *and* TALC *re-enter carrying wood. This time
they've got* GINGER *following* TALC. *He walks
just behind him, with ominous power. He doesn't
say anything.*

FIZ    And I said to her, yeah, well, you've got a vagina
no one would want, and she said, yeah, I know.

TALC    Yeah?

FIZ    And so I said – thinking I'll enjoy this as a bit of
an experiment – science experiment – you know
– mating habits of the dumb – why not make a bit
of an effort.

FIZ, *without acknowledging or even seemingly
noticing him* (*she doesn't turn around*) *hits*
GINGER *hard in the balls with the back of her
swinging hand. He crumples.* TALC *and* FIZ
*keep walking.*

You've got some tits on you. Use them. Cover up
the spots. I introduced her to mascara. Mainly for
the science experiment, you know? She's only
pregnant now.

GINGER *stumbles off.*

TALC    Is she?

FIZ    Seven weeks.

LOPPY *walks past them in the opposite
direction, he's wearing large 1970s hearing aids.*

LOPPY    Alright.

FIZ    Alright.

TALC    Alright.

LOPPY    (*Singing.*) Alright.
Alright.
Alright.

*He walks on.*

FIZ      I ask her who the dad is – she says 'one of five' – I say that's what mascara will do for you – she says, yeah, brilliant, but Mum won't let me have an abortion. I said, I don't have an answer for that, Debbie – Debbie Debbie Debbie. And she said, I didn't expect you to.

*They put the wood down.*

RICK      How much more you got to bring?

FIZ      Not much of a story.

TALC      No. But, you know, I still liked it.

FIZ      This is the last piece. Mr McKendrick is looking for you…

RICK      Is he?

FIZ      Well, I say looking, not hard, I mean, if he was looking – hard he'd come up here, because this is where you'll always be, but he asked us to pass on a message, which is that you're to look for him, when you've got a chance, when you're not up here, which is likely to be never, so this is probably pointless. Are teachers allowed to take their tops off?

RICK      I'm not your teacher.

FIZ      Isn't a bit – you know – inappropriate. Not that you've got much of a body. So any untoward thoughts I might have had – about a teacher with his top off – I'm unlikely to have had about you – because you with your top off? Not so much. Just so you know.

RICK      Okay. Thanks.

FIZ      I play it as I see it. I find life is easier that way. Or if not easier certainly more straightforward. And besides – teacher-student relationships never turn out well I've heard. You want me to go find McKendrick? Return the – you know – the message.

RICK　　No. You're okay.

*There's a pause. He looks at them.*

So – what would you like to do next?

FIZ　　We done our bit now, sir, helped you out – best
we could – we'll go back to watching you being
a lonely prick now if that's okay.

RICK　　Oh. Okay. Sure.

FIZ *looks at him, and then back out at the
audience.*

FIZ　　(*Singing.*) Imagine the scene:

*The* KIDS *run around and get ready to play
parts. They do as this story develops. Playing
shop-owners and mothers and thieves.*

Imagine the scene –
Mum takes you down the shop
She's looking for a mop
You steal a box of screws
And nails you'll never use

You nick a bag of chips
Mum sees and she just flips
You're grounded for a week
She treats you like a freak

The chips have turned to mush
But it gave you such a rush
You have to take some more
It's lifted life's long snore
This is the best bit of my day.

KIDS　　They tell you life is for the living
You get more when you're giving
They say be what you can be
Fuck off this is me
I say fuck off this is me
And my life is boring
Boring.

GINGER          Imagine the scene:

                *They run around and assemble a class.*

                You're sitting in maths class
                Spitting on some paper
                You aim at Toby's arse
                Wrapped-up spit is safer

                The teacher is a prat
                He thinks he's where it's at
                He grabs you by the scruff
                He starts to treat you rough

                He throws you out the door

                *The* KIDS *grab him.*

                You slide across the floor

                *They throw him hard down the back of the stage,*
                *they get a little too in to it.*

                (*Spoken.*) Fuck off. Whoever did that. Fuck off.

                *He thinks and then looks up.*

                (*Singing.*) Maths book is left inside
                He calls you something snide
                This is the best bit of my day.

KIDS            They tell you life is for the living
                You get more when you're giving
                They say be what you can be
                Fuck off this is me
                I say fuck off this is me
                And my life is boring
                Boring.

DEBBIE          Imagine the scene
                You're hanging with some bloke
                He thinks it's just a joke
                He tries to grab your tits
                You knock him in the bits.

FIZ             (*Spoken.*) Jesus, Debbie, you have to go full
                porno, don't you?

*They arrange into pairs, only there's not enough
girls, so* GINGER *and* LOPPY *end up together.*

GINGER    Oi. There's been a mistake. There ain't enough
women.

DEBBIE    (*Singing.*) The park is full of tins
They've burned down all the bins
Sitting in the stench
Kissing on a bench
Is this the best bit of my day?

KIDS      They tell you life is for the living
You get more when you're giving
They say be what you can be
Fuck off this is me
I say fuck off this is me
And my life is boring
Boring.

TILLY     Imagine the scene.

HIGGY     Imagine the scene.

TALC      Imagine the scene.

LOPPY     Imagine the scene.

KIDS      This is the truth
They can't deny
Our life is shit
And we know why
It's cos we're kids, we're best ignored
Left at the back, and safely bored
Mom says 'what can I do with you?'
We shrug back saying 'we ain't a clue'
Our life is boring, safely boring
Always boring, fucking boring, boring.

          FIZ *turns to the audience.*

FIZ       Okay. To start at the – I mean, he is the
beginning, and I'm really sorry about that,
because in terms of first impressions – you know,
he comes across as a bit of a knob.

RICK *is standing at the front of the school beside a projector. They sit on, at or near chairs. This is an assembly hall.*

RICK     Hi. I'm Rick. Rick Davies.

*The rest of the cast turn and mimic him perfectly.*

ALL      Hi. I'm RICK. RICK Davies.

FIZ      One of those teachers who thinks we'll really – you know – respect him on his – you know – level if he – you know – encourages us to use his – you know – first name.

*RICK thinks and then rethinks his stance.*

RICK     If it'll make you more comfortable you can call me Mr Davies.

*He smiles. He puts down a slide on the OHP, he puts it the wrong way around, he readjusts it. It's of a Junk Playground.*

But I'd rather you didn't. My mother called me Richard. So you can call me that too. But Rick is the name I will answer to. Nothing rude too. If you can… Nothing rude too.

*He laughs. He checks if anyone else is laughing. They aren't.*

Some of you may know me for a bit of fill-in I did for your maths class a few weeks back. But you probably won't. I was the guy with his feet on the desk, a book in his hand and poetry in his head. Or…

I'm reading a lot of C.S. Lewis at the moment – finding some parallels. You know. To life. And – you know. Anyway.

*What is he saying? He doesn't know. No one else knows either. He shuffles.*

I just want to read you a little bit from Lady Allen – my ultimate boss – not met her but she's – um –

she set up the London Adventure Playgrounds
Association – which is an old name – we're
aware this isn't London – we're not in London
any more, Toto – that's a – that's – *Wizard of Oz*
joke – she set up LAPA – which I work for.
Anyway, she wrote 'how does an Adventure
Playground differ from the usual playground?

(*Singing*.) There is no asphalt,
no see-saws,
no swings or slides –

*He stops singing, but he starts drumming, the
drumming continues under the rest of the speech.*

– except those created by the children themselves
out of waste material freely available on the site
or by the terrain of the playground itself. The
main difference is that –

(*Singing*.) – the children are given facilities
which are the spur to their creative abilities –

*He stops singing.*

– and to their love of fun and inventiveness…
The Adventure Playgrounds described here are
intended for children between the ages of six and
eighteen who want, in addition to a rough
playground, to have the opportunity of doing
tough jobs of real work that will stretch their
abilities to the full.

So – yeah. They have employed me – just a guy –
from Walthamstow – to work with you on
building a playground. Of wood. And your
headmaster has allowed me to come today to talk
to you about why I want to do it and how I want
you to be involved…

Which is I want you to be involved in everything.

Which is that this playground will mean nothing
unless it's built by you.

FIZ          Now, I'm not a joiner-in. Ask my mum.

             *A light turns her on* FIZ's MUM *who is elevated
             above the stage.*

MUM          No one likes our Fiz. She's quite peculiar.

FIZ          That's not the bit I meant, Mum...

MUM          She don't help herself by only bathing once a
             fortnight. I told her, if her friends wanted friends
             who stank of fish they'd go live in an acquarium.

FIZ          Where did that come from? I actually wash.

MUM          You know, every first day of school, whatever
             I said to her she'd always go in, register, and then
             walk straight out again and come home to me.
             And I tell you one time... at the fête.

FIZ          Mum. Mum. Stop, okay?

             *Light clicks off on her* MUM.

             The fête was. Well, to cut a long story short,
             I was selling bags of popcorn, as a six-year-old,
             and I accidentally shit myself.
             You see? Did you need to know that? No.
             It was quite traumatic actually.
             And what kind of mother brings that up? What
             kind of mother thinks the fact that I shit myself is
             relevant to you people?
             I don't fit in well.
             Well. I did fit in well. And then it all got... And
             I've got friends. I've got Talc.

TALC         Me.
             Yeah.
             I'm her...
             I'm her friend.

FIZ          Anyway, so yeah, I didn't want to join in. On the
             whole playground business. But then none of us
             did. Partly because Rick was a prick.

'I'm reading a lot of C.S. Lewis at the moment –
finding some parallels. You know. To life. And –
you know. Anyway.'

Partly because, you know, who'd want to join in
building a fucking playground? We're thirteen
years old. The fuck we want with a playground?
And they don't even want to give us a GOOD
ONE. They want to give us a shit one. Out of
junk. In fact, worse than that, they want us to
build it for ourselves.

So it became a sort of spectator sport. Watching
him. Building stuff.

*Music begins. And we flip and we're out of the
classroom and back at the playground.*

*The junk orchestra starts to play a rhythm –
which sits underneath this whole scene.*

*There's a sort of weird rumba feel to it.*

And it was quite fun. Watching him... Not in a...
I mean, he's not a... I mean, look at him. But
that's what made it fun. Watching someone good
at making stuff is not fun. Watching someone
bad. I mean, that's the entire plot of *The
Generation Game*.
And he was. Crap.
And it was fun watching him being – crap.
I thought about selling popcorn.
I didn't.

| | |
|---|---|
| TALC | What's he building? Is that going to be a slide? |
| FIZ | I don't think so. |
| TALC | A diving board? |
| FIZ | No. |
| TALC | A ladder? |
| FIZ | No. |

TALC      What's it going to be then?

FIZ       He's building a sort of – thing.

RICK      (*Singing*.) I'm building a thing.
          I'm the king.
          Of this thing.
          That I'm building.
          Won't you join in?
          Be a king.
          Of this thing.
          With me?

FIZ       I think he thought – initially – that he'd set an
          example of how much fun it'd be and that we'd
          all join in the fun.
          Then he realised we were having better fun
          watching him.

TALC      What is that?

FIZ       So he started to get – desperate.
          He got the school to promise us certificates if we
          were to get involved.
          Yup. Certificates. They're always a winner.

RICK      (*Singing*.) It's starting to expand.
          Won't you lend me a hand?
          We'll be quite a band.
          It won't be grand.
          But it could help you land
          A university place.

FIZ       We said…

HIGGY     (*Singing*.) Fuck no.

LOPPY     (*Singing*.) You're alright.

HIGGY     (*Singing*.) Fuck no.

TILLY     (*Singing*.) We don't give a fuck about uni-ver-
          ver-ver-sity.

FIZ       And he wouldn't give up.
          Even though we showed no interest whatsoever.

RICK        (*Singing*.) Look it a grow.

            *He inflates a balloon with 'Grand Opening'
            written on it. It ascends into the air.*

            I don't want to crow.

            *He inflates a balloon with 'Second Grand
            Opening' written on it.*

            But don't you know
            What this could be

            *He inflates two balloons which he twists together
            into a swan on the front of which says 'Third
            Grand Opening'.*

            If you just agree
            To become a we
            With me
            This guy from Walthamstow.

FIZ         He threw a wine and cheese evening because he
            thought the sophistication would appeal to us.

RICK        Juice and cheese. Juice and cheese evening.

FIZ         He tried.

RICK        I tried.

FIZ         He tried.

RICK        I tried.

FIZ         Everything.

RICK        (*Singing*.) Come on, guys
            Keep your eyes on the prize
            This is about the future.
            This is about –
            This is about –
            (*Spoken*.) Come on, guys.

## Scene Three

FIZ*'s house. There's a sofa, a telly, and not much else.*

NEWS ANCHOR
        The rubbish mountain in Leicester Square grew
        yet higher today as Westminster Council
        continued to use the location as an official dump
        site. Protests in Liverpool, Manchester,
        Newcastle and Bristol continue. Prime Minister
        Callaghan's office have released no official
        statement other than to say that inflation is the
        enemy and they will not put the national
        economy's growth at risk in order to curb the –

        FIZ *gets up and changes the channel. She changes
        it to* The Kenny Everett Video Show, *the theme
        music blares out uncomfortably. Then she changes
        it again. To* Life on Earth.

        *Her* MUM *comes back in holding a cup of tea.*

MUM       Weren't we watching the news?

FIZ         It finished.

MUM       Did it?

        *She checks her watch.*

        That's a – funny – thing for it to do – it's six
        twenty-two.

FIZ         They got bored talking. They said 'and now over
        to – ' and then they just stopped, looked up at the
        camera and said 'I can't even finish this sentence
        this is so boring.' They put on some cartoons
        instead. It was most unexpected.

        MUM *looks at* FIZ, *she sighs.*

MUM       Oh.

FIZ         And this has got animals in it. So, you know...

        DEBBIE *comes in and sits down – she's now
        noticeably pregnant.*

DEBBIE     What's this?

MUM     Animals.

DEBBIE     Why?

FIZ     Why animals?

DEBBIE     Yeah?

FIZ     Why animals? As in why do animals exist?

DEBBIE     Mum.

FIZ     This from a girl that kept a rat in a box.

MUM     Fiz.

FIZ     What?

MUM     You know, what...

FIZ     How's the bump?

DEBBIE     I don't know. It's still here.

FIZ     You're going to be a brilliant mother.

DEBBIE     Mum.

MUM     Fiz.

FIZ     (*Singing.*) Neil.

Neil was a boring man.
He'd want news followed by news.
He'd want lager followed by lager.
He'd scream and he'd shout about what
was wrong.
And then fix none of it.

My home.
Is a tale of three women.
My home.
Into which brave and not-so-brave men roam
And then run away again.

Jim.

DEBBIE      (*Laughing*.) Oh Christ, Jim.

            (*Singing*.) Jim was a morning man.
            He'd make eggs followed by eggs.
            He'd ask questions followed by questions.
            We thought he cared, and wanted us fat.
            He was eight months and out.

            My home.
            Is a tale of three women.
            My home.
            Into which brave and not-so-brave men roam
            And then run away again.

FIZ         (*Spoken*.) Tim.

DEBBIE      Tim!

MUM         Not Tim.

            MUM *joins in too*.

            (*Singing*.) Tim was a nasty man.
            Knew when to land a punch.
            Punch on Friday never on Monday.
            Because then it faded – be faded by work.
            He kicked Deb and was gone.

            My home.
            Is a tale of three women.
            My home.
            Into which brave and not-so-brave men roam
            And then run away again.

            *The doorbell rings.*

            *They look at each other.*

            *The doorbell rings again.*

            MUM *stands and sighs and walks from the room.*

            DEBBIE *looks at* FIZ *who looks back.*

FIZ         Animals?

DEBBIE      I'm gonna kick your head in.

            MUM *re-enters with* RICK.

*They all look at him, quite scared. Quite astonished. But primarily scared. But* MUM *puts a brave face on it.*

MUM          Look who's here…

FIZ          Mr Davies?

RICK         Hi. Sorry. To interrupt. Your evening.

MUM          Do you drink tea?

RICK         Sorry?

MUM          Am I saying it wrong? Tea? Do you drink it?

RICK         Yeah.

DEBBIE       I'll get it.

             DEBBIE *bolts from the room.*

RICK         Debbie, isn't it?

             *She turns.*

DEBBIE       Yeah.

             *She continues to bolt.*

RICK         Hi.

FIZ          You said that.

MUM          Will you sit? It's just a sofa I'm afraid.

FIZ          What do you think he normally sits on, Mum? A throne?

             RICK *sits.*

             *He looks at them expectantly. They look back at him – more expectantly.*

RICK         Great sofa.

             *He thinks.*

MUM          Well…

RICK         Yes.

| | |
|---|---|
| MUM | Do you eat biscuits? |
| RICK | I can't stay. |
| MUM | (*Shouts off.*) Debbie, bring the biscuits. |
| FIZ | He's not staying. |
| DEBBIE | (*Off.*) Okay. |
| MUM | (*Shouts off.*) And not the broken ones. |
| FIZ | Good. This can't get worse. Good. |
| MUM | We don't have teachers round very often. Ever. We've never had a teacher in this house. We don't get many visitors at all. To be. Honest. |
| RICK | Well, I'm here on a recruitment mission. |
| MUM | Are you? |
| RICK | I want Veronica to be – um – |
| FIZ | Fiz. I'm called Fiz. She called me Veronica… |
| MUM | She's named after Veronica Lake. A beautiful woman. |
| FIZ | Who died alone after battles with mental-health issues and alcoholism… my name is Fiz. |
| RICK | Which I will call you, if you call me Rick. Anyway, Fiz, I'm here to recruit you… |
| MUM | She'll do it. |
| FIZ | You have no idea what it is! |
| MUM | She's good at maths. She's less good at history. If you can find a use for her… |
| RICK | Oh, I'm not looking for academic students, I'm looking for leaders, and your daughter she's a leader. |
| MUM | She's a what? |
| RICK | She's a leader. |
| MUM | Fiz? |

*Four boys start to gently sing in the background.*
FIZ *steps forward.*

GINGER        (*Singing.*) He told me mum I had integrity.
              I didn't know what it meant, she did, she smiled.

TILLY         (*Singing.*) He told my mum I was charming.

HIGGY         (*Singing.*) He told my mum I was funny.
              She tried to hit me, he said he meant it in a good
              way, she beamed.

TILLY         (*Singing.*) He told my mum I was charming.

LOPPY         (*Singing.*) He told my mum I had potential.
              You should have seen her grin.

TILLY         (*Singing.*) Charming. Me. My mum.

TALC          (*Singing.*) My mum wasn't home.
              He said he wanted me to join in, I said okay.

FOUR BOYS *and* TILLY
              (*Singing.*) My mum.
              My mum.

FIZ           I'd have told him to fuck off if it wasn't for the
              fact that when he said it – well, my mum – her
              face lit up. He was a clever bastard.

FOUR BOYS (*Singing.*) My mum.
              My mum.

TILLY         My mum.

FIZ           But her face lit up, and so I was doing it. He hit
              four of us that night. Four of us the night after.
              The clever bastard.

TILLY         (*Singing.*) Clever bastard.

FOUR BOYS *and* TILLY *and* FIZ
              (*Singing.*) Clever bastard and my mum.
              Clever bastard and my mum.
              Clever bastard and my mum.
              Clever bastard and my mum.

FIZ          There were probably failures along the way. But, you know, he had his team. The clever bastard.

*And slowly our junk orchestra is brought into play. Slowly we see the full might of what is possible on this stage.*

*And, I won't lie to you – the stage swings a little.*

## Scene Four

*And the stage is full of* KIDS *lifting, building, and making. We hear bits of the following.*

HIGGY        I'm actually going to put your dick in a jar.

TILLY        You are not lifting it, Ginger.

FIZ          To explain who a few of us are…

GINGER       I am lifting it.

FIZ          Ginger is, well, Ginger. He wants to be on TV when he's older. Luckily he doesn't really mind if it's *Police 5* or not.

GINGER *raises a finger at her.*

GINGER       Funny funny funny.

LOPPY        And then she said something about me and algebra. Which I'm not – well…

HIGGY        I'm putting it in a jar and I'm gonna put rose petals inside and then I'm going to sell it as a fucking paperweight.

TALC         Okay.

TILLY        I am lifting all of it, Ginger.

GINGER       Give a bit. Give a bit.

FIZ          Loppy is – well part-philosopher, part-twat, part-*Guinness Book of Records*. There isn't any record he hasn't attempted. The pogo-stick one got quite nasty.

LOPPY    And then Mam said she weren't having breakfast for saying that. I mean, I'm not even tall.

GINGER    Give a bit.

TILLY    I'll give you a lot if you're not careful.

FIZ    Higgy is really interested in the law. Specifically Crown Court. He has developed the habit of nicking wigs just to see how he looks in them. He looks good.

RICK    Well, will you look at that.

GINGER    Now, I'm lifting all of it.

TILLY    Give a bit.

FIZ    And Tilly – well Tilly got born a girl. And she's hated that fact ever since.
We're a bunch of junk really. Well, I say junk, cunts is an equally valid way to call us. Little annoying cunts.

LOPPY    So she hit Mam. I mean, I do have a bit of a neck on me.

HIGGY    A quid. Two quid. I'll give it away for nothing. I'm calling it a 'Dick in a Jar with Rose Petals'. It'll be art. I'll cut you in.

TALC    Okay.

RICK    Everybody. Listen up.

TILLY    Who you actually talking to, Loppy?

LOPPY    What?

TILLY    Who you actually talking to, Loppy?

LOPPY    Talking doesn't actually need to be 'to' someone. You'll learn that.

HIGGY    (*In the style of Scottie from* Star Trek.)
Aye aye, Captain.

| | |
|---|---|
| RICK | Everybody. If you could. |
| TILLY | You're a lazy mare, Ginger. |
| HIGGY | 'A Dick in a Jar.' It'll catch on. |
| TALC | Okay. |
| TILLY | Just lift some of it, Ginger, yeah? |
| FIZ | WILL YOU ALL PLEASE LISTEN TO RICK? |
| | *Everybody turns.* |
| RICK | Uh. Thanks. Fiz. |
| FIZ | You got to make them listen, they won't listen if you don't make them. Okay. Go – |
| RICK | I just want to thank you all for being here. It means a lot. It's overwhelming. I just wanted to say – thanks. |
| | *Beat.* |
| FIZ | That all you got? |
| RICK | Yup. |
| FIZ | Well. I was hoping for better than that. |
| GINGER | (*The bass line.*)<br>Clever bastard<br>Clever bastard<br>Clever bastard<br>Clever bastard<br>Clever bastard. |
| | *And then the* KIDS *sing over the top – building the playground as they do.* |
| KIDS | (*Singing.*) My mum. The things I do – for my mum<br>Who is a little bit dumb<br>My mum.<br>Who is not a Yummy Mummy<br>Not even the slightest bit scrummy<br>My mum. My mum. |

Making shit with wood – for my mum
Because she gets quite glum
My mum
Around men she's a mess
She fucks and gets depressed
My mum. My mum.

HIGGY's *thumb spurts blood*.

HIGGY      Fuck, my thumb.

(*Singing*.) My mum. I give thanks – for my mum
She's the best thing about this slum
My mum
She gives me dinner most days
She even tries to give me praise.

GINGER     And I'm a wanker

That is my mum.

## Scene Five

MALCOLM's *office*. RICK *is talking to* MALCOLM.

RICK       I've got to say I'm excited.

MALCOLM    And we – at the school – are also very excited.

RICK       I feel like we're reaching out to the kids, finally.

MALCOLM    You're reaching out and it's very impressive.
           I just want to warn you –

RICK       I'm warned. Consider me warned.

MALCOLM    That some of these students aren't necessarily.
           Some of these students are not necessarily our
           best students.
           And I want you to be aware.

RICK       I'm entirely aware.

MALCOLM   That some have problems with things that they're
          instructed to do.
          That lad, John Whiting.

          GINGER *pops up in the scaffold.*

GINGER    John – who?

RICK      Ginger.
          The kids call him Ginger.

MALCOLM   He's in and out of care.

GINGER    I am.

          LOPPY *appears above, swinging down on a*
          *piece of piping.*

MALCOLM   His mother is a prostitute – she tries to look after
          him as much as she can but –

RICK      I've been to the house, I've met her.

MALCOLM   His brother has a history of violence and has been
          in and out of borstal. John is showing every sign
          of following him.

LOPPY     That true, Ginge?

GINGER    Mind your fucking business.

MALCOLM   And that girl Matilda Bagshaw.

TILLY     He's starting on me now.

MALCOLM   A history of abuse. An uncle. No one knew it
          was happening. Three years, from the ages of
          seven to ten.

TILLY     My mum bottled him when she found out.

MALCOLM   Need I go on? I mean, young Tom –

TALC      Please don't talk about me.

RICK      I'm aware, Malcolm, I am.

MALCOLM   Everyone – everyone here, they've all got dark
          stories. And they need best standards of care. We
          all do – we may not seem it – but these kids
          matter to all of us.

RICK  But imagine if – imagine if we can unlock them – I mean, the possibilities of it – we can really achieve something and make them feel like they've really achieved something.

MALCOLM  Bit of caution. That's all I'm saying.

RICK  Received and understood.

FIZ  But he didn't receive it and he certainly didn't understand it.
The thing about Rick is…

GINGER  The thing about Rick is…

HIGGY  He really just wanted to build a playground.

GINGER  And the other thing about Rick is…

TILLY  He made us want to build one too.

RICK  (*Singing*.) When I was a child I liked building dams
I built them all over Hackney
When I was a child I liked building dams
In streams, in sewers, in puddles on the floor.

FIZ  When I was a child I liked blah blah blah
Blah blah blah blah I'm bored are you?
When I was a child I liked building blah
Blah blah blah blah blah blah blah blah blah.

RICK  Wood can be anything.
FIZ  Wood can be nothing.
RICK  Look at what I'm making.
FIZ  You're making shit.

RICK  When I was a child I did loads with wood.
FIZ  You would. You would. You fucking would.
RICK  When I was a child I liked using nails.
FIZ  Well screw you, screw you, screws are best.

RICK  When I was a teenager I liked making camps.

FIZ *and* GINGER
You dirty skank, you must have stank like a tramp.

RICK                When I was a Ranger Scout the children built
                    their own.
                    When children build together they are never alone.

FIZ, HIGGY *and* GINGER
                    (*With a grin.*) You sound like a massive paedophile
                    Doing nasty stuff to children
                    You bore me, you scare me,
                    I think I might have to report you.

RICK                This playground can be anything you want it to
                    This playground must be something built by you
                    I just want your minds free, to let them roam
                    To know this is your family, this is your home.

KIDS                The playground is an open sewer
                    I don't know why I like it.
                    I don't know why I'm part of it at all.

ALL                 Wood can be anything
                    Wood can be nothing.
                    Look at what we're making.
                    Come and join in.


**Scene Six**

*The* KIDS *are gathered, having a brainstorm.* RICK *watches
a scaffold, smoking, keeping a careful eye on them all.*

TALC                I've got this idea involving a swing that's
                    attached to a roundabout.

HIGGY               Yip yip yip.

TILLY               (*Ignoring* HIGGY.) Sounds good.

TALC                And you have to swerve around iron spikes as
                    you're swung.
                    We could call it – I don't know –

FIZ                 – The Impaler.

| | |
|---|---|
| HIGGY | One of them splash rides. You're strapped in a box and you're like thrown in the river. |
| LOPPY | Dead Cat. We should call it a Dead Cat. |
| FIZ | Only problem – we ain't got a river. |
| LOPPY | We can make a river. |
| HIGGY | I'll be a fucking river. |
| GINGER | Hey, Tilly, I'm a river, you're a river, am I making you wet? |
| TILLY | Go fuck a duck. |
| TALC | We should do a Demon Dragon Ride. |
| HIGGY | Yip yip yip. |

FIZ *moves around the group towards* HIGGY.

| | |
|---|---|
| FIZ | Demon Dragon? |
| TALC | It needs a mouth and a tail and a lot of petrol. Essentially you're on a rope and the ground is on fire. |
| HIGGY | Yip yip yip. |

FIZ *lamps* HIGGY *in the balls. She knows he's taking the piss out of* TALC. *He crumples.*

| | |
|---|---|
| FIZ | Maybe the rope should be on fire too? |
| TALC | Okay. Yeah. I mean, nice. |
| TILLY | A sweat cage. Which you're locked in and then there's fire on all sides. |
| FIZ | Dragon fire. Double-use. |
| LOPPY | A human hamster wheel. |
| FIZ | That could be on fire too. |
| TILLY | A wing extending high in the air – like a bird's buried – |
| TALC | Like an angel's buried. |

TILLY        An angel wing. I like it.

GINGER       Three bikes suspended six feet in the air that
             you're strapped to and you got to keep peddling
             otherwise they'll crash down on the floor. But the
             thing is it's not just you got to keep peddling –
             it's everyone – all three of you. So you're
             shouting – keep peddling – at all the other riders.
             My brother'll sort us the bikes.

TILLY        A pit. We just dig a hole in the ground and see
             how deep we can go.

HIGGY        And if we can't find use for it, it'll be great as
             somewhere for Ginger's brother to bury the
             bodies.

             GINGER *looks at* HIGGY, *he doesn't like that.*

TILLY        The pit. The whole hole. The – something.

GINGER       Higgy's Anus. We call it Higgy's Anus.

FIZ          I reckon the dragon idea is the best.

TALC         Demon Dragon.

HIGGY        Dragons are pussies.

GINGER       Hey. I've got it. A phone exchange.

             *Everyone stops, surprised.*

TILLY        A phone exchange?

GINGER       A thing you can talk to other people through.

HIGGY        You want to talk to people, Ginger? What you got
             to say?

GINGER       Fuck you.

             GINGER *gets to his feet,* HIGGY *gets to his feet.*
             RICK *makes to move down to them, but then*
             *stops himself.*

LOPPY        Anyone else think this meeting is getting a bit –
             angry?

GINGER       Anyone else think Higgy's a bit of a dick?

HIGGY       You're the dick, you called the big hole thing my
            anus. I ain't got a big anus.

GINGER      And I ain't interested in doing this if people ain't
            gonna do this properly.

TILLY       Who ain't doing it properly? You asked me if
            I was wet?

            *And now everyone is on their feet, this meeting
            isn't going well.*

GINGER      A phone exchange is a great idea.

HIGGY       My thumb up your arse is a great idea.

FIZ         I reckon the dragon idea is the belter.

LOPPY       I liked the human hamster wheel.

GINGER      I'm gonna fucking start hitting people soon.

TILLY       Maybe they'll hit you back.

            RICK *starts to move towards them, decisively
            this time.*

            *But then,* DEBBIE *walks past them in the
            opposite direction, her pregnant belly sticking out
            in front, she must be five months now. There's
            instant silence.*

            RICK *sits down again.*

DEBBIE      Hello, Talcum Powder.

TALC        Okay. I mean, yeah. I mean, I'm... I mean, hello,
            Debbie.

DEBBIE      Fiz.

FIZ         Fatty.

DEBBIE      (*Singing.*) James – a massive potato.
            He looked – like a massive potato.
            I kissed him – because I wanted him to be –
            grateful.
            He was nice.

Making the same mistakes as Mum
That's what I do
And I have no clue
Why I do.

Ben – with big bad eyebrows
Squishy face – with huge eyebrows.
I kissed him – because he asked me to go –
dancing
It was nice.

Making the same mistakes as Mum
That's what I do
And I have no clue
Why I do.

Phil – with the really spotty back
Looked ready – to erupt that back
I tugged him – because I thought he liked me
He did not.

Making the same mistakes as Mum
That's what I do
And I have no clue
Why I do.

Dave – with the scrappy scraggly beard
He looked – dirty with that beard
I blowed him – because my mate dared me to
Then he laughed.

Making the same mistakes as Mum
That's what I do
And I have no clue
Why I do.

Ginger, Pete, Higgy, Greg with the –
Dirty, mainly dirty, smelly –
I did them because it seemed right to
And that was that.

I got this.

*She touches her belly.*

Making the same mistakes as Mum.
That's what I do.
And I have no clue.
Why I do.

DEBBIE *walks on past* GINGER. *The* KIDS
*scatter in all directions on the playground.*

DEBBIE      Piss off, Ginger.

GINGER      Did I say anything?

HIGGY       Alright, Debs.

DEBBIE      Go swivel, Higgy.

FIZ         What just happened there?

TALC        She just talked to Ginger, who I think is still
            pretty angry about the phone-exchange idea.

GINGER      It's a great idea.

FIZ         Is it because I told you that she was easy?

TALC        What?

FIZ         You. With Debbie. Then.

TALC        I only said hello. I was honestly quite surprised
            she said hello to me. We'll be alright, right? I
            mean, I know the meeting didn't go well but
            that's just people steaming off, ain't it? Give it
            some time and...

FIZ         You've got a crush on my sister, haven't you?

TALC        What? No.

FIZ         Don't lie to me, Talc, I can always tell when you're
            lying. You start shedding skin. You're crushing on
            my sister? You think about her in a romantic sense?
            In a wanking sense? Oh my God, you think about
            my sister when you masturbate. I'm not sure what
            to say. What to imagine. What to do. I might have
            to stab you for her honour and stab myself to stop
            the thoughts of you masturbating playing again and
            again through my head.

| | |
|---|---|
| TALC | I don't… |
| FIZ | You do, don't you? Oh Talc, why? Why why why why why? |

*There's a hesitation.*

| | |
|---|---|
| TALC | I don't fancy your sister. |
| FIZ | If you get married and have deformed children with my sister, I will drown them all at birth. |
| TALC | I don't fancy her because…<br>I don't fancy her because…<br>Doesn't matter. |
| FIZ | I don't believe you. |

*TALC looks at her.*

| | |
|---|---|
| TALC | That doesn't matter either. |

### Scene Seven

| | |
|---|---|
| FIZ | And then came…<br>And then came…<br>And then came the first attack…<br>Well, I say attack it was hardly…<br>I mean, the Nazis didn't suddenly arrive and beat the crap out of everything.<br>It was more…<br>It was more. Well…<br>One man and his stolen kettle full of stolen petrol.<br>But it's amazing what damage a stolen kettle full of stolen petrol can do…<br>Dragon. |

*Part of the stage ignites behind FIZ. GINGER, TILLY, LOPPY and HIGGY appear within it, singing.*

| | |
|---|---|
| GINGER | (*Singing*.) But we hadn't finished. |
| TILLY | (*Singing*.) We weren't done. |

*The fire grows.*

| | |
|---|---|
| HIGGY | (*Singing*.) You can't burn something half-made. |
| LOPPY | (*Singing*.) That really isn't fair. |
| FIZ | (*Spoken*.) I mean, we hadn't even finished anything and this kid... Or man... |

*TALC runs on with a bucket of water, he throws it on the flames.*

Or woman...
When none of us were there...
And it meant...
And the playground burnt...

*The KIDS pass buckets of water between them.*

*The fire is extinguished.*

And actually – it was quite sad.

| | |
|---|---|
| RICK | It's okay to be sad. |
| GINGER | The motherfuckers. |
| RICK | Okay. Maybe not that sad. |
| GINGER | The cunts. |
| RICK | Yeah. Definitely not that either... |
| TILLY | I really like what we'd done, is the problem. |
| RICK | We can rebuild. |
| GINGER | Revenge first then rebuilding. |
| HIGGY | Aye. |
| RICK | Can we find out who did this? If we can then I'd like to know? |
| GINGER | I'll find out. |

FIZ            Lock up your daughters and your nans, Detective
               Ginger is on the prowl.

GINGER         Nans. I'm not interested in nans.

TILLY          (*Singing*.) Oh give us a loan
               Of your toothless old crone girlfriend
               I'll make her groan
               If you give me a loan
               Of your toothless old crone girlfriend.

               GINGER *raises a finger at her aggressively.*

               What you gonna do?

RICK           Look, guys, I understand you're upset, I'm upset,
               you're upset.

HIGGY          We're all upset.

GINGER         I actually am upset, is no one else actually upset?

FIZ            Everyone's upset.

GINGER         (*Indicating* HIGGY.) Then why does he sound
               like he's not upset.

FIZ            Because he struggles with sincerity since he lost
               his virginity.

HIGGY          I want to kill them too, okay?

LOPPY          Kill them? Did he say kill them?

HIGGY          It'll probably be the kids from the rec. Why don't
               we start there?

TILLY          Bit of torture.

GINGER         Am I the only one taking this seriously?

RICK           Without wanting to see any violence, I would like
               to know who they are.

FIZ            Anyway that was – I mean, it was…
               The burning of the Angel Wing was the…
               Because we did security rotas after that.

GINGER         And I made weapons.

FIZ            And Ginger made weapons.

GINGER         Using some tools – hammers, spanners,
               wrenches.

FIZ            B&Q didn't know what hit 'em. He stole
               everything.

GINGER         Some sticks.

FIZ            He picked those up in the woods.

GINGER         And some small cloth bags.

FIZ            CW Seconds for the cloth bags.

GINGER         It's amazing what damage you can do with a bag
               of nails.
               On a rope.

               *He demonstrates, swinging a bag of nails around
               his head.*

FIZ            Ginger's quite scary when you get to know him.
               And he did his investigation.
               His armed investigation.
               And he seemed okay at it.

RICK           Ginger... Ginger...

               *He grabs him and takes him to one side.*

               I need your word you won't – it's important to
               me there isn't actual violence, you understand?

GINGER         Yeah. No. Completely understand.

RICK           I mean it...

GINGER         This is just for show. They know it.

RICK           What?

GINGER         (*Singing.*) I remember very clearly
               My first visit to a pub
               My brother was all cheery
               We even had some grub.

               *The* KIDS *join in with some 'ahhs' underneath.
               He looks at them all glaringly, they start to sway.*

But then it went
A little bit wrong
But then it got
A little too strong
Cos fighting is how you belong.

*He turns around angrily.*

(*Spoken.*) Shut the fuck up. I mean it, next one to
sing under my song gets it.

HIGGY          You got it, mate.

GINGER         (*Singing.*) My brother got all leery
               With a girl who looked quite hot
               She was nice and beery
               But her man was clearly not.

That's when it went –

*The* KIDS *join in underneath with 'ahhs'. He
looks around angrily, they all raise a finger at him.*

A little bit wrong
That's how it got
A little too strong.

(*Spoken.*) Pricks.

(*Singing.*) He beat her man black and blue
He could have killed him if he wanted to
He looked at me like I should have been proud
I was not.

*He looks at* RICK.

(*Spoken.*) You got my word, sir. No fists.
Nothing.

RICK           Okay.

GINGER         Violence makes me sick, to be honest. But, you
               know, people like to think – I'm – you know –
               and I – you know – don't like to disappoint them.

RICK           You're quite a surprising guy, you know that?

GINGER     Not even naturally ginger, sir. Dye my hair.

RICK       Really?

GINGER     Fuck off! Who'd dye their hair ginger? I'll get
           you some names, sir. You do what you want with
           them.

FIZ        And while Ginger did his searching – we did our
           little security thing. We protected the site. We
           protected the playground.

           *A torch flashes across the stage. And then
           another. And then another.*

HIGGY      Who goes there?

TALC       Who is that?

HIGGY      Loppy – that you?

LOPPY      Who goes there?

FIZ        We did security.
           It brought us together.
           Security. We protected our site. Twenty-four
           hours a day. We were a team. We wouldn't be
           fucked with.

TALC       Who goes there?

           *A sheep baas.*

## Scene Eight

RICK *is showing* MALCOLM *around the playground.*

MALCOM     And this will be?

RICK     We call this The Ship's Hull.

MALCOM     And what do you do on a ship's hull?

RICK     .     Uh, well, I guess um –
You climb it. You stand on it.
It's not so much about what you do on it, more
about –

TALC     You sit in it.

RICK     Thanks, Talc. Yes, you sit in it.

GINGER     You sail it?

RICK     It's about creating an imaginative space,
Malcolm.

MALCOLM     Mr McKendrick amongst the children, please.

RICK     Sorry. Mr McKendrick. It's about creating an
imaginative space.

MALCOLM     And it is. It does seem to be. It does seem to be
that. You know, we were pressured quite hard by
the Council to consider this as a new maths
block. But this is – this is quite something…

FIZ     The headmaster visited on the twenty-fourth day
of the rebuild. Mainly because Ginger had
stopped going to classes and when he did turn up
he was covered in sawdust. Partly because he was
– you know – intrigued.

MALCOLM     Inspired and intrigued.

FIZ     Intrigued and inspired and scared.

MALCOLM     Scared?

FIZ     Anyway, Rick put a shirt on and everything.

MALCOLM     Intrigued because I never thought I'd get you kids
involved in anything.

FIZ            He's okay, but he does call us 'you kids' with the
               same vocal tone as someone would say 'you
               cunts'. Which, and I hope I've been clear on this,
               we do entirely deserve. All the same...

MALCOLM    Inspired because this is the sort of – I like the
               way this reaches out to the community of – to the
               community of you – kids.

FIZ            (*To audience*.) Yup.

MALCOLM    Scared because – did I use the word scared? No.
               Not scared. Inspired and intrigued.
               Congratulations, Rick.

RICK          Thank you.

MALCOLM    And this is – is this finished? What will be here?

GINGER      The Spider.

MALCOLM    And what will you do on The Spider?

GINGER      You're like a fly. You get caught in its web. The
               idea is you slowly starve to death. In it. On it.
               Attached, you know? Unable to get away. Caught.

MALCOLM    Right. And this will be?

FIZ            The Death Hole.

RICK          Fiz...

MALCOLM    And what do you do on The Death Hole?

FIZ            It's an imaginative space in which you might die.

RICK          Fiz. Not entirely. Not entirely helpful.

FIZ            Am I lying? It's called The Death Hole. We
               called it The Death Hole.

RICK          It's a provisional name.
               You fall through it. Or slide down on it,
               depending on your preference.

FIZ            And you might die.

GINGER      Yeah. You might die.

MALCOLM *pulls* RICK *aside*.

MALCOLM   It's quite extraordinary how quickly you've managed to rebuild.

RICK   It won't be called The Death Hole.

MALCOLM   It doesn't matter to me what you call it, what concerns me more is the fact that it was burnt down in the first place...

RICK   Just kids playing.

MALCOLM   And the fact that you're looking for the kids who did it.

RICK *realises the real purpose of* MALCOLM*'s visit*.

RICK   Not personally I'm not.

MALCOLM   John Whiting.

GINGER *pops up*.

GINGER   John – who?

RICK   Ginger.

MALCOLM   Has been all over the Lockleaze and St Paul's estates telling people he's trying to find out who did it for you.

RICK   He promised he wouldn't use violence.

MALCOLM   Whether or not you should trust his word...

RICK   I believe I can trust his word, there's no 'should' about it.

MALCOLM   You're risking inflaming a delicate situation.

RICK   I know what I'm doing.

MALCOLM   And if you find who did this, what do you intend to do about it? Take them to the police?

RICK   No, I'll try to recruit them of course.

MALCOLM   You'll enlist them?

RICK            The only way to engender cooperation from the
                kids is to work with them. That's what the Junk
                Playground Movement is about...

MALCOLM   You'll enlist – arsonists – to work with wood-
                building?

RICK            You should see the changes in these bunch of
                guys. I believe...

MALCOLM   It's not about what you believe, Rick, it's about
                what's practical. I've instructed John Whiting to
                stop his search and I want you to do the same.
                Do I have your word?

RICK            Yes.

MALCOLM   And that is a word I choose to trust.

                *He looks back at the playground.*

                It truly is wonderful to look at. Such imagination.
                Death Hole. Wonderful.

                *Elsewhere onstage,* TALC *is sawing into some
                wood.*

                GINGER *is hammering some nails into a pole.*

GINGER       Any trouble last night?

                TALC *says nothing.*

                You were on last night, right? Any trouble last
                night?

TALC           Are you talking to me?

GINGER       Does it look like I'm talking to you?

TALC           It's more than possible you are.

GINGER       I'd say it was probably pretty definite, don't you.

                *Beat.*

TALC           It's just you never talk to me.

GINGER       That's because you're a shithead who stinks
                of cum.

TALC        That's the way I've understood it too.

            *Pause. They go back to their tasks.*

GINGER      I don't know why I'm talking to you either.

            *Pause.*

            But any trouble last night?

TALC        Yes. No trouble.

GINGER      Good. That's the last thing I'll ever say to you.
            Good.

TALC        Okay then.

            *Pause.* GINGER *looks at* TALC. *Two musical
            saws start a duet in the background.*

GINGER      You're going with the grain. You're sawing with
            the grain.
            That's not good you know...

TALC        I'm not very – they said they wanted some planks
            – I told them I couldn't do it.

GINGER      You can do it, you just got to look at the wood.

            *He picks up* TALC*'s piece.*

            Can you see the grain?

TALC        Yes.

GINGER      The grain'll squeeze you. Fuck you right up and
            your saw. So you gotta cut against it.

TALC        Right.

            *He starts again.*

GINGER      Right. Come here. Stay still. Do you see?

            *He leans over* TALC *and helps him saw.*

            It's easy, do you see?

TALC        Yeah.
            Yeah.

**Scene Nine**

| | |
|---|---|
| FIZ | With no more interruptions… |
| TALC | With no more interruptions… |
| GINGER | Things moved quick. |
| FIZ | We built quick. |
| LOPPY | We learnt all woodwork stuff. Butt joints and… The only one I can remember the name of is butt joints. But there were others. |
| RICK | It's done. |
| LOPPY | Loads of others. Butt joints and… |
| RICK | Can't you see? It's done. |

*They turn and look at it.*

*And you know what, it is done.*

*This strange and beautiful construction.*

| | |
|---|---|
| GINGER | Well, would you… |
| HIGGY | Look at that. |
| TILLY | The Death Hole is the best bit… |
| TALC | No. The Spider. |
| HIGGY | No. The – what's that one? |
| FIZ | That's the one Ginge wants to call Bondage Master but Rick said no. |
| RICK | I think there has to be a line – and – |
| HIGGY | Bondage Master, I like it, it's catchy. |

*They all say nothing.*

*They just look at their Junk Playground.*

*As it dominates the stage.*

| | |
|---|---|
| TILLY | (*Singing.*) This is a Spider, this is a ship This is the thing where we do dip-the-dip |

We haven't quite worked out what this thing is
But we promise you it is the biz.

*There's silence, they all smile.*

(*Spoken.*) It's good. That's what it is – it's good.
We done something good.

FIZ    And – so – what do we do now?

*There's a pause.*

TILLY    Time to show it to the world don't you think?

LOPPY    Party – we need a party.

FIZ    And after that? After the party?

GINGER    We protect it. It's ours.

## Scene Ten

*It's raining.* RICK *and* FIZ *sit underneath The Ship's Hull.*

RICK    (*Singing.*) When I was a child I liked
building dams
I built them all over Hackney
When I was a child I liked building dams
In streams, in sewers, in puddles on the floor.

FIZ    When I was a child I liked blah blah blah
Blah blah blah blah I'm bored are you?
When I was a child I liked building blah
Blah blah blah blah blah blah blah blah blah.

*They smile at each other.*

RICK    Fag?

FIZ    Again, you see, you're reaching past the point of
appropriateness. You may think it's cool – do you
understand the word cool? You may think it's
'hip' – do you understand hip – of course you
understand hip look at your trousers – to offer

a student a cigarette – but – and I promise you this – the practice is widely frowned upon.

RICK    I'm offering a colleague a fag.

FIZ    Colleague? Is that supposed to make me feel all warm and fuzzy inside? Because it doesn't. I'd rather you respected the pupil-teacher boundaries.

RICK    Okay. I'm having a smoke.

*FIZ nods. RICK lights a cigarette.*

FIZ    Go on then. Give us one.

RICK    It's probably inappropriate.

FIZ    You offered me!

RICK    And then you showed me the error of my ways and I realised that the pupil-teacher boundary is a sacred boundary.

FIZ    If you don't give me a cigarette I'll tell the McKendrick that I went to you with help with my period and you told me it was dead natural and then helped me insert my first tampon.

*RICK grins and hands her a cigarette. They both smoke.*

Why are you here, sir?

RICK    Why am I literally here? Because we were working on the site and the rain came down and we had nowhere else to go.

FIZ    I meant...

RICK    I know what you meant. Why are you here?

FIZ    I'm here because you bullied me into it. It's a fucking playground. It's a terrible waste of my time. But your time, you could have a proper job. Work in a café – anything...

RICK    True.

FIZ    And Ginger asked the McKendrick who told him you were paid very little.

| RICK | (*Laugh*.) Why did he tell him that? |
|------|-------------------------------------|
| FIZ | He wanted us to feel sorry for you I think. I think he thinks your job is an absolute waste of time too. |
| RICK | He undoubtedly does. |
| | *Beat.* |
| FIZ | He says you've got a degree.<br>He said to us, do you know that he's got a degree? |
| RICK | Yes. I do. |
| FIZ | He said it like – do you know he's got a degree and still he's doing this shit? |
| RICK | I can imagine. |
| FIZ | So why are you doing it? Is it because you don't want a proper job? |
| RICK | I like what we're doing here. |
| | *Beat.* |
| FIZ | Are you proud? |
| RICK | Of what? |
| FIZ | Of this thing? |
| RICK | I'm really proud. Are you proud? |
| FIZ | Can I ask though… what's the point of it? What's it for? |
| RICK | Can I reverse the question? Can I ask – what do you think the point of it is? |
| FIZ | No. You can't. I asked you. |
| RICK | I think the idea is that it's somewhere you kids can feel like kids again… |
| FIZ | That sounds terrible. That's a terrible thing to say. Never tell anyone else you ever said that. |
| RICK | What should I say instead? |

FIZ         That you just wanted to build something and so
            did we.

RICK        That's actually... I really quite like that.
            You know when I was your age I just wanted to
            play football all the time.

FIZ         Oh God, were you a prick, sir?

RICK        I mean, all the time. I was pretty decent. A pretty
            decent player. Got into a decent youth team.
            But I wasn't – it turned out – I wasn't good
            enough to play – football.
            And that made me – hate it – football.
            And when I looked around – the people I'd grown
            up with – when I looked up from the football thing
            – I mean, it was my focus, my life...
            And by the time I looked up – they were into
            drugs, or in borstal, or somewhere else. I thought
            football ruined my life. But it saved it.

FIZ         Which youth team? Which youth team did you
            play football for?

RICK        Watford.

FIZ         And you think you were good?

            RICK *laughs*.

DEBBIE      Talc, you seen Fiz?

            TALC *becomes visible sitting on the scaffold.*
            DEBBIE *is beside him, neither can see* RICK *or*
            FIZ. *The rain has now stopped.*

TALC        Oh, hi, Debbie. No, Debbie.

RICK        Good point.
            My point is...

FIZ         You want to save us.

RICK        No...

FIZ         Save us like we are people out of depth in the
            sea. Save us like we're rhino, or African

|        | penguins. I mean, without this I'm destined for prostitution. You know it. I know it. |
|--------|--------|

RICK       That's (unfair)…

FIZ        You think your football-type philosophies can focus us and save us from a life of drugs and crime. I thank you for your knight-ish behaviour.

RICK       The headmaster wants me to tell Ginger to stop looking for the kids who burnt the playground…

*FIZ kisses RICK.*

*He pushes her away.*

FIZ        What? I was playing the princess – thanking the knight. Giving him my – favour, they call it a favour, don't they?

RICK       I don't know, I wasn't ever very good at history.

FIZ        Don't look so scared. I won't tell no one. Just thought we needed to kiss.

RICK       Fiz, you are aware that – you are aware that –

DEBBIE     Fiz! If you don't come out from where yer hiding right now!

FIZ        You're not interested in me.

RICK       I'm interested in your mind. But you're a girl. You're just a girl.

FIZ        And there was me thinking you thought I was more than that.

RICK       And I'm a grown man.

FIZ        Don't forget, I seen you with your top off, sir, if that's a man I'd ask for your money back. I've got to go.

DEBBIE     Fiz. FIZ. FIZ. Mum wants you home. FIZ. Fuck!

FIZ        Got to go. Don't tell her I was here.

*She pulls herself up on to the top of The Ship's Hull.*

*She stops at the top.*

Sorry.

RICK      No. I'm sorry. I'm sorry you got the wrong idea – you're a smashing girl.

FIZ      'Smashing.'

RICK      No, no...

*With tears pricking her eyes, she disappears, as* DEBBIE *rounds the corner.*

DEBBIE      You seen my sister?

RICK      Yeah. She was just here. She said not to tell you she was here.

*RICK looks at her, there's a pause.*

DEBBIE      I hate her.

RICK      She's a bit – upset.

DEBBIE      How come you never asked me to help with your playground?

RICK      I did. In assembly.

DEBBIE      You asked all the other mums. You didn't ask mine. Or you did ask mine – but not for me.

RICK      I didn't think you'd be in to it.

DEBBIE      Don't worry, you ain't alone, no one ever asks me to do much.

RICK      You – no, I just...

*She looks at* RICK.

DEBBIE      Boys, I mean... boys. Or men. Or whatever you are.

DEBBIE *exits.*

RICK *is left alone.*

RICK            (*Singing.*) When I was a child I liked
                building dams
                I built them all over Hackney
                When I was a child I liked building dams
                In streams, in sewers, in puddles on the floor.

                *Beat.*

                (*Spoken.*) Shit.


### Scene Eleven

*The stage is in total darkness.*

*Suddenly a torch runs on to the stage. Or a person holding
a torch.*

*Then the torch goes out.*

GINGER          Shit.

                *The torch is hit once, twice, three times, it briefly
                glows into light and then dies again.*

                Shit.
                Fucking.
                This is the sort of shit that...

                *A lighter is lit. A cigarette is lit. The cigarette is
                smoked.*

                *The torch is hit again. It works suddenly.*

                *It's pointed in four directions.*

                Wherever you are. Wherever you are.

                *Then it alights on something.*

TALC            Ginger...

GINGER          Oh shit. Oh shit.

                *The torch dies again.*

TALC        I... I...

GINGER      Guys! Guys! Oh shit. Oh shit.

            *He runs, he trips, he falls, he hits at the torch. It's not giving off anything now.*

            Guys. Guys! GUYS!

            *The lighter is relit, to pick out the prone body of FIZ, he makes his final way over to her.*

TALC        She was here – and I was frightened – and then she was – she sent me away from her – by –

GINGER      Oh shit. Oh shit. Fiz. Fiz. Fiz. Can you hear me? Fiz. Guys. It's FIZ. Fiz. Fiz. Look at me. Look at me.

            *The lighter goes out.*

            *Then a lighter is lit elsewhere in the theatre.*

            *Then another one.*

            *Then another.*

            *Suddenly there are eight lighters lit.*

            *And then a hum starts.*

TILLY       There is a blackbird
            Sitting
            On a black post
            In the dark.
            You may not see it.
            But it's there.

            There is a black tar
            Oozing
            In the darkness.
            Slinking in.
            Like the worst nightmare
            It is here.

            Night.
            It's the best time of the day.
            It's black. It's dark. It's secret.

*And as she sings,* FIZ*'s body is lifted up and
away.*

There is a person
Standing
Just behind you.
Hugging you
With their darkest arms
Tightly close.

Night.
It's the magic time of day.
It's just. You can't. See what's there.

Courage sits
Waiting
In a cave.
It's got no friends.

*Interval.*

## ACT TWO

### Scene One

TALC *is sitting alone.*

TALC          (*Singing.*) The muffled sounds
              I find a comfort
              The way they sit
              Outside my head

              I like the noise
              Of a life outside
              It makes me feel
              It's okay out there

              Sometimes I hear
              Some things that frighten
              Sometimes I hear
              Some things that scare me

              But then I shut my ears
              And I sing this song
              Then I refuse to hear
              What Mum says.

DEBBIE        Hey…

              TALC *stops singing and turns, surprised.*

              DEBBIE *is now seven months pregnant.*

TALC          Hey.

DEBBIE        How did you, uh…

TALC          They said that they weren't supposed to be…
              They said no one was supposed to be up here.

DEBBIE        So why are you up here?

TALC          Cos they said that no one was supposed to be up
              here and I wanted to check.
              They put iron round the locks.

| | |
|---|---|
| DEBBIE | They did. I know. |
| TALC | But the fence is pretty low to climb over.<br>So I thought... I'd check...<br>In case anyone else had the same thought.<br>I wasn't expecting you to have the same thought.<br>You're pregnant. |
| DEBBIE | I am pregnant. |
| TALC | And that is...<br>Well, then that's quite impressive.<br>Climbing over that fence. When you're pregnant.<br>I struggled. And I don't have the belly issue. |
| DEBBIE | No. |

*Pause.*

| | |
|---|---|
| TALC | Do you want to sit down? |
| DEBBIE | And do what? |
| TALC | And do whatever you came up here to do. |
| DEBBIE | What are you doing – up here... |
| TALC | Sitting. Protecting. Nowhere else to be really.<br>So just sitting. Protecting. |
| DEBBIE | So you're offering me – you're saying I can sit<br>with you and protect with you? |
| TALC | Well...<br>I wasn't.<br>Yeah. If you like. |

DEBBIE *sits beside* TALC.

Can I ask you a question?

| | |
|---|---|
| DEBBIE | Long as it's clean. |
| TALC | Who's the dad? |
| DEBBIE | Ginger. |
| TALC | Really? |
| DEBBIE | Yeah. I know. Bit surprising he's capable of it.<br>Fatherhood. But he is. At least the biological bit |

of it. Or Higgy. It could be Higgy too. Or someone called Ken, but he was really drunk so I don't think it was.

TALC        So you don't really know who the dad is?

DEBBIE      No. Can I ask a question?

TALC        If you like.

DEBBIE      Why do people call you Talc?

TALC        BO issue. I thought talc was the answer.
            I was wrong.

DEBBIE      Fiz used to get called fish for the same reason.

TALC        I remember.
            It's sort of how we became friends.
            Well, not really.
            It's sort of the reason why I thought we should be friends.
            And I sort of just followed her around until she agreed.

            *Pause.*

            You know, it's sort of…
            What I've been thinking about most today.
            Who is, and it's stupid because I should have been thinking about Fiz.
            But I can't stop thinking about my auntie today.
            She was a bit ill. She's dead now. But she was always a bit ill.
            And one time – our only real holiday my mum took me to her mum and dad's.
            They lived in Weston-Super-Mare. Have you been?

DEBBIE      Yeah.

TALC        You have?

DEBBIE      I went with school.

TALC        Oh. Yeah. I couldn't go on that trip. Didn't have the subs.
            Anyway, we went there for a few weeks – five weeks actually – one summer, I missed the first

week of school and then Mum got a call and we
came home.

Mum was just – there'd been problems with a man.
I forget his name.

(*Singing*.) Anyway, my auntie –
Auntie Rose,
Aunt Rose –
because she was a bit ill she always stayed with
her mum and dad –
had always stayed with her mum and dad.
She'd had time in mental hospital but other than
that she'd always stayed with her mum and dad.

Her mum and dad.
Mum and Dad.

(*Spoken*.) She loved me – my Aunt Rose – you
know how you can tell? You can tell that people
just love you. She loved me. I was ten.
Every day we'd take a walk. She'd never say
much. But we'd walk down to the beach and back,
because I loved the sea and the sand. I'd never
seen the sea before and I loved it. And – um –
we'd go down and we'd kneel on the sand and
every day we'd build a sandcastle. Not a big one.
Just one to show we were there. And then we'd
watch the sea for a bit and then we'd go home.
And by the time we came back the next day the
sandcastle would be gone and we'd build a new
one. You know, it was our way. And Mum didn't
mind. My mum didn't get on with her mum and
dad. My mum mostly sat in the garden fagging.
The week we got back. And I was quite happy to
leave because I was worried about missing school
and getting further behind. Because I don't like to
be behind. And I wanted my bed back. Mum got
a call, the week we got back, my Auntie Rose had
hung herself.
She was dead.
And I always thought that if I'd been there, it'd
have never happened.

That's the thought I couldn't get out of my head.
But I know now – if I had been there – it'd have
happened all the same.
Because I wouldn't have made a difference.
She told me to leave her alone – she was crying –
she never liked to cry in front of other people –
your sister – said she had a blackbird flying round
her head – in her head – a blackbird in her head –
and so I had to leave her alone. But I wasn't far
away. And when I heard her – her scream – I came
running as fast as I could. But by the time I got
there they was gone.
And she was just lying there.

DEBBIE    I don't think I've ever seen her cry.

TALC    No?

DEBBIE    Not since she was six or something.

TALC    She was quite private about it – crying.

DEBBIE    Yeah.

*Pause.*

You did all you could.

TALC    And that's nice to say – nice of you to say – but
the truth is – if I'd been someone else – maybe
what I could have done would have been better.

DEBBIE    I know you've come to the hospital.

TALC    Yeah.

DEBBIE    The nurses said you're very polite. They said
there's a scrawny lad comes in. Very polite.

TALC    Sounds like me.

DEBBIE    My mum said she saw you one time when we
were in. Said you ran away. Said she wouldn't
mind if some time you came and sat with us.

TALC    That's kind too…

DEBBIE    Not really. She's just got nothing to say and
there's all this pressure because the nurses say

she might be able to hear. And you know how
difficult it is to keep Fiz interested.

TALC          Yeah.

DEBBIE        Mostly we just have the radio on. And sit holding
one of her hands each. What do you talk about?
I bet you talk loads.

TALC          No. Mostly I just sit too.
I don't even hold her hand.
I should have thought – I should do that.
I will remember to do that. Next time I'm in.

              *Pause.*

DEBBIE        Ginger's trying to find who did it, you know that?
Says he's going to find who did it and make them
pay. Dunno how you pay for Fiz though, right?
I mean, she's dead expensive, ain't she?

TALC          Yeah.

DEBBIE        Talc.

TALC          Yeah?

DEBBIE        Can I hold your hand? Now I mean.

TALC          Yeah.

DEBBIE        Just for a bit.

TALC          Yeah. Just for a bit.

              *And he looks at her hand.*

**Scene Two**

FIZ*'s living room.* RICK *sits on the sofa uncomfortably.*

FIZ*'s* MUM *enters carrying a coffee.*

| | |
|---|---|
| MUM | Two sugars. I put two sugars in. I wasn't sure if you asked for one or two sugars and so I thought I'll put two in, because you can't really – I've always thought you can't really have enough sugar. I've always thought that – really – everyone who asks for one sugar really wants two. |
| RICK | I wasn't sure whether to come. |
| MUM | It's good that you did. Debbie's out. It'd have only been me. I'm not sure I'm ready for just me yet. |
| RICK | Do you know where she is? |
| MUM | No. Does that make me a bad mother? They always did. Go wherever. I should probably think about stopping that happening now. Considering. |
| RICK | No. |
| MUM | Maybe she's gone to the hospital. Visiting hours are long since over. We've got nothing to say to her anyway. We normally put the radio on. Or I tell her what I've heard on the radio. It's not much of a conversation. |

RICK *says nothing.*

How many sugars do you normally take in your coffee?

| | |
|---|---|
| RICK | This is fine. |
| MUM | How many sugars do you normally take in your coffee? |
| RICK | I don't take any sugars. |

*Beat.*

And I asked for tea.

*Beat. He smiles at her. She smiles, briefly. And then sits on the sofa.*

| | |
|---|---|
| MUM | I quite fancied you. I'll be honest, I quite fancied you when you first came over. |
| RICK | Thank you. |
| MUM | You're not actually – you're not actually that much younger than me – I've just got kids. But there's not such an age gap. |
| RICK | No. |
| MUM | You didn't fancy me though? |
| RICK | I didn't even – it's sort of frowned upon – teachers dating their pupil's parents. It's sort of discouraged. |
| MUM | You're not a teacher. You're a playground attendant. |
| RICK | True. |
| | *Beat.* |
| MUM | Why are you here? |
| RICK | Now? |
| MUM | Why are you here? I'm trying to figure it out. |
| | *(Singing.)* Maybe you want me to forgive you<br>Maybe you want a bounce<br>Maybe I want that too<br>If what I want counts. |
| | *(Spoken.)* Anxiety – fear – sitting by your daughter's bedside trying to work out whether she'll die or not – is actually – it actually does – make you a bit horny. But it's not that. So is it the forgiveness thing? And what exactly am I forgiving you for? |
| RICK | I wanted to – I wanted to check you were okay. |
| MUM | Did you think I would be? Okay? Because I'd say that's unlikely, don't you? |

RICK        Yes.

            *Beat.*

            Yes.

            *Beat.*

            Yes. I think I probably am here for forgiveness?

MUM         I'd rather you were here for a bounce.

RICK        Yes. I'm not. Here for that.

            *Pause.*

MUM         Which bit do you want forgiveness for?

RICK        Well. Uh. I'm not sure.

MUM         She was up there protecting your playground.
            They gave her a beating because she was
            protecting your playground. She wouldn't have
            got hurt at all without your playground. Maybe
            that? And maybe – maybe – the fact that she
            shouldn't have been up there – at night – on her
            own – unattended.

RICK        She wasn't supposed to be alone. That lad Talc
            was supposed to be on with her – though it's not
            his fault – she asked to be alone – because she was
            upset – and – the reason why was upset was – me.

MUM         How did you upset her?

RICK        On the afternoon before – she'd tried to kiss me –
            we'd been alone – and I'd made clear that it was
            inappropriate and that I didn't – wouldn't –
            couldn't reciprocate her feelings.

MUM         She tried to kiss you?

RICK        Yeah.

MUM         She fancied you too then.

RICK        Seems that way.

MUM         Just like her mum.

RICK          And I think I could have dealt with it better –
              I was going to talk to her in a couple of days –
              but of course – the timing couldn't be worse.

MUM           I'm not going to forgive you.

RICK          No.

MUM           Fuck you and fuck your playground.

RICK          Yes.

              (*Singing*.) I thought I was doing a good thing
              I thought I was changing things
              I thought I was making people sing
              But instead I was making them cry.

MUM           My home.
              Is a tale of three women.
              Into which brave and not-so-brave men roam
              And then run away again.

RICK          Sorry.
              It seems a stupid word.
              Sorry.
              It seems a crap thing to say.
              But sorry.

GINGER        (*Spoken*.) I was the first to hear about it.
              My brother has a – he has the sort of radio which
              picks up the police radio.
              It helps him sometimes.
              The call came through – about an attack going on
              at the Lockleaze Junk Playground.
              They actually used the whole phrase 'Lockleaze
              Junk Playground'.

TILLY         I don't really like calling it playground.

GINGER        Apparently Talc – not wanting to leave her alone
              – just screamed beside her until someone came.

RICK          (*Singing*.) Sorry.
              It seems a stupid word.
              Sorry.
              It seems a crap thing to say.
              But sorry.

TALC        (*Spoken*.) I didn't see their faces.

GINGER      Talc didn't see nothing. They'd gone before he
            got there.
            But I'm going to make it my business to find out
            who was up there.
            I'm going to find out who did this, you
            understand?

MUM         (*Singing*.) My home.
            Is a tale of three women.
            Into which brave and not-so-brave men roam
            And then run away again.

RICK        I thought I was changing their worlds
            I thought I was challenging their souls
            I realise now what a prick that makes me
            I just made them cry.

MUM         Rick was a funny man
            Thought he knew what we were
            You're this. You need this.
            But he was worse than all the rest
            Wish he'd never come round.

RICK        Sorry.
            It seems a stupid word.
            Sorry.
            It seems a crap thing to say.
            But sorry.

MUM         My home.
            I don't want it to be a tale of two women.
            Please.
            Not a tale of two women.
            Please.

            *And then we hear a 'beep beep' of a machine.*

            *And* FIZ *is revealed in intensive care.*

## Scene Three

MALCOLM *approaches her bedside.*

*He looks at her carefully.*

TALC *comes back into the room, holding a packet of beef crisps.*

*They're both are slightly shocked to see the other.*

MALCOLM  Hello.

TALC     Hello. Sir.

MALCOLM  Just here for a visit.

TALC     Okay.
         I'll just um… I'll just um – go.

MALCOLM  Is this your coat?

         *He indicates a coat on the chair beside her bed.*

TALC     Yes. It is.

MALCOLM  So you were already here…

TALC     Yes. I was.

MALCOLM  So it is I that is intruding on you.

TALC     Yes. I think.
         I don't know.
         I think I'll go all the same.

MALCOLM  You just went to get some beef crisps…
         I didn't know you were allowed to eat beef crisps
         in intensive care.

TALC     They say to be – they say to be – careful. As long
         as you don't get crumbs on the equipment.
         They say it's okay. A nurse bought them for me
         actually. Said I looked hungry.
         Which I was. A bit.
         Sorry. Still speaking. Bit nervous.

MALCOLM  No need to be nervous of me.

TALC          I'm not nervous of you, I'm nervous she'll die.

              *Pause.*

MALCOLM   I'm just here on behalf of the school really.

TALC          That's good.

MALCOLM   To say – I'm just here to say – on behalf of the
              school – how sorry I am.

TALC          Okay.
              Am I supposed to accept it? Your sorry? I don't
              think I should.
              They say she can hear actually. So maybe you
              should say it to her.
              Not that – she would say – not that you have
              actually anything to be sorry about.

MALCOLM   Okay then.
              Well, I think I might say it anyway.

              *He sits. He looks at* FIZ.

              Sorry.

              *He thinks.*

              Well, that's all I really…

TALC          Okay.

MALCOLM   See you soon, Tom.

TALC          Are you going to close it? Are you going to close
              the playground?

              *Beat.* MALCOLM *looks at* TALC *softly.*

MALCOLM   Sometimes you have to make difficult decisions –
              Sometimes it's just about protecting kids in
              danger
              Sometimes it's about prioritising that –
              She shouldn't have been there, son.

              MALCOLM *leaves.*

              TALC *stays.*

              *We stay with him.*

TALC          Okay then.
              Okay.
              So what do we talk about now?

              *There's a pause.*

              (*Singing.*) I don't fancy your sister. I've never
              fancied your sister.
              Because…
              Because I fancy you…
              Well, not fancy, fancy is the wrong word.
              Because I can't think of any other girl other
              than you.
              Not that I fancy you.
              Because that's the wrong word.

              *There's a pause.*

FIZ           (*Spoken.*) What you're saying is…
              You love me…

              TALC *looks at her surprised.*

TALC          You're okay?

              FIZ *sounds and should continue to sound
              incredibly weak. But she fights the weakness hard.*

FIZ           I'm guessing so.

TALC          I need to fetch someone.

FIZ           Fetch who?

TALC          A doctor or something.

FIZ           I'm in a hospital, am I?

TALC          Yes. You're in a hospital, you've been out four
              days, you're okay, I hope, you were attacked, up
              by the playground and…

FIZ           Oh, okay. I've never stayed in a hospital before.
              I always thought the first time would be when
              Debbie popped the kiddie out. I win, Debbie.

TALC          Shall I get a doctor or a nurse?

FIZ           Not yet.

| TALC | I feel like I need to… |
|------|------------------------|
| FIZ | I can move my arms – I can move my legs – you're okay. |
| TALC | Can you remember anything? |
| FIZ | I'll be honest, I sort of woke up, while the McKendrick was here, but I didn't want to interrupt your juicy and meaningful conversation. Yes, I remember things. |
| TALC | We're supposed to get the police as soon as you – |
| FIZ | Don't. Oh, I am feeling quite – |

*Pause.*

Yeah. You should probably get a doctor.

*The beeps start to get louder again.*

## Scene Four

*And then suddenly all the* KIDS *are around the bed. Above it, below it, across from it, placed on the playground.*

| HIGGY | You said to them 'fuck off' and then they lynched you. |
|-------|------|
| FIZ | Thought they was just up there to burn it down. They weren't. |
| GINGER | And you remember nothing of 'em? |
| FIZ | No. I remember some things. Remember their smell. I just can't remember their faces. I probably didn't see their faces. |
| GINGER | Have you tried drawing their faces? |
| FIZ | No, cos I can't remember their faces. |
| TILLY | He's going to ask why you didn't use one of his socks full of nails in a minute. |

| | |
|---|---|
| LOPPY | Anyway, the doctors have given you the all-clear – your head's all sound and that. |
| FIZ | I mean yeah, I sometimes speak in Chinese, but other than that – all good. |
| GINGER | But you remember their smell. What did they smell of? |
| FIZ | Piss and cigarettes. |
| TILLY | Well that narrows it down to every boy in Bristol. |
| FIZ | Anyone else bored of talking about me? I am well bored of talking about me. Can we talk about something else please. |
| HIGGY | Cos of this, everything has gone to shit. You know that, right? |
| LOPPY | Playground's coming down. |
| FIZ | Talking about the playground also is a bit boring, but okay. |
| TILLY | An' I don't really like calling it a playground. |
| GINGER | They got in professionals. They're taking it to bits. |
| | *The playground starts to be dismantled around them.* |
| TILLY | Walled us out. Big wire fences. Like a prison, but the other way round. |
| HIGGY | And Rick has total disappeared. |
| | *A light lights on another part of the stage.* |
| RICK | I'm anxious to make a new start in life. I've actually recently acquired a girlfriend, which is a forward-step. And I'd consider working as a resource manager in your esteemed team a forward-step too. And I'm excited about stepping forward. |
| MALCOLM | The decision was made – by the school governors – who are all good people by the way. |

*The* SCHOOL GOVERNORS *stand up from
behind the playground..*

SCHOOL GOVERNORS
(*Singing.*) We are all good people by the way.

MALCOLM   To return the land to what everyone thought it
should be used for. Which is – a maths block.

SCHOOL GOVERNORS
(*Singing.*) A maths block would be very nice.

HIGGY   You seen him? Rick?

FIZ   Yeah. The hospital had to put him up for the night
actually – give him a bed – wouldn't leave my side.

LOPPY   Yeah?

FIZ   No. Didn't even come when I was sick. Couldn't
give a fuck. Never did. We were just a job for him.

GINGER   Yeah?

RICK   Previously? Well, as you can see from my – CV –
I've been teaching…
I've been working with – teaching – at-risk kids.
Which I think makes me perfect for work in the
probation service. And some of their brothers and
sisters were in jail already I think – so, you know –
that might give me a head start – getting to know –
your 'clientele'.
Sorry, I'm not sure why I mentioned the girlfriend,
really. She's very nice, she's called Alice.

MALCOLM   The playground – was unsafe. It was that simple.

SCHOOL GOVERNORS
(*Singing.*) The playground is unsafe. It's that
simple.
And so it must be closed.
Closed.
Closed.
And maths. Maths needs support.

TILLY   Anyway – most days – we've been bunking off
and going and have a watch.

GINGER      Four of us, five of us, just sitting – watching.
            You should come up.

SCHOOL GOVERNORS
            (*The singing is swinging now.*) Two, three, five,
            seven, eleven, thirteen, seventeen
            Maths needs support.

FIZ         Where?

GINGER      The playground.

FIZ         No. You're okay.

RICK        Yeah. It was a playground, but I don't want you
            to think of it – actually think of it as maybe
            leading – the idea was to lead the children – but
            I got a lot out of it too –
            We were trying to involve kids in making
            something. Being part of something.
            And now I want to be part of your work in – in,
            um... in, um...

SCHOOL GOVERNORS
            (*Singing.*) Nineteen, twenty-three, twenty-nine,
            thirty-one, thirty-seven, forty-one
            Maths
            Maths
            Maths needs support.

HIGGY       Come on. Come up the playground. Tilly'll make
            some soup –

            TILLY *raises a finger in his direction.*

            – we'll make a day of it, watching them do their
            thing.

FIZ         Don't you understand? I don't want nothing to do
            with that place.

HIGGY       What's going on with you?

FIZ         你不明白吗？我不想和那个地方做任何事 (Nǐ bù
            míngbái ma? Wǒ bùxiǎng hé nàgè dìfāng zuò
            rènhé shì.)

| RICK | Yeah. There was some – trouble.<br>It's going to be a maths block now. So a new start for the school and a new start for me.<br>Which is why I'm here. For my new start. In the world of museum archaeology.<br>If you'll have me. This is the museum archaeology job, right? |
|---|---|
| GINGER | Come on. Come down. We won't leave you alone. No one's getting to you, Fiz. I promise you that. |
| FIZ | It was bollocks though. That's what I've realised – lying here – what we did – it was bollocks – just a distraction thing for kids no one knows anything else to do with – it meant nothing. And I want nothing to do with it, ever again. |
| GINGER | No. You're wrong. |
| FIZ | I'm not, and you'll work it out yourself some day. |
| GINGER | (*Singing*.) My brother once built a skateboard<br>It went quite fast<br>But he was nice when he asked<br>And I ended up with two broken legs<br>Plastercast. |

*And as it is sung so the playground dismantling speeds up.*

*And* FIZ *just watches. And as the platform is taken down below her:*

| HIGGY | My sister once dressed me in lace<br>I felt really quite nice<br>I put snail shells in my hair<br>She put bleach powder all down my front<br>Plastercast. |
|---|---|
| RICK | (*Spoken*.) I'll be honest with you, sir. I've always wanted to be a – (*Reads from a piece of paper*.) legal librarian. And in terms of seeing my CV as a – I've always been interested in knowledge – the dispensing of knowledge. |

ALL        (*Singing, apart from* FIZ.)
           This was a Spider, this was a ship
           This was the thing where we did dip-the-dip
           We haven't quite worked out what this thing was
           But we always thought it'd be the biz.

TILLY      My uncle once built me a teepee
           I loved it in there
           It was quiet and he cared
           But when they found us they shouted
           Plastercast.

RICK       (*Spoken, with no passion at all.*) Town planning
           is my utter passion. Yes. I've always wanted to be
           a town planner. It's a fascination with two things,
           planning and towns. I know my CV hasn't led me
           here. But to be honest, what's gone before is not,
           in my case, a sign of what's to come.

ALL        (*Singing, apart from* RICK.)
           This was a Spider, this was a ship
           This was the thing where we did dip-the-dip
           We never quite worked out what this thing was
           But we always thought it'd be the biz.

RICK       You will? You do? Well, that's fantastic. That's
           absolutely fantastic. Great. Town-planner Rick.
           Richard. Richard the town planner. I like it!

FIZ        (*Singing.*) My friends and I worked on a
           playground
           We thought it was great
           We thought it'd had fixed us.
           But it was…
           It was…
           Plastercast.

## Scene Five

| | |
|---|---|
| RICK | Hello, Talc. You waiting for me? |
| TALC | Yeah. |
| RICK | Why didn't you knock? |
| TALC | I got too much respect for your privacy, sir. |
| RICK | You been out here long? |
| TALC | About three hours. I weren't sure what time you got up in the morning, and I thought – to myself – maybe he gets up at six – because some people do – I've heard – who lead busy lives – so I set my alarm and got here for six – but it turns out you don't get up till nine, sir, so... |
| RICK | Aren't you freezing? |
| TALC | That doesn't matter. How come you won't see Fiz? |
| RICK | That's a – complicated question – |
| TALC | She's okay now. It weren't all your fault. It was actually mostly my fault. So you should go see her. |
| RICK | I don't think she wants to see me. |
| TALC | I think she does. |
| RICK | I don't think you know that. |
| TALC | I think I do. |
| RICK | Well, then we'll agree to disagree. |
| TALC | No, we won't. |
| | RICK *looks at* TALC. |
| RICK | Your lips are blue, can I get you a cup of tea at least? Warm you up a bit. |
| TALC | When I was little, whenever my mum got a bit – like she gets – I used to hide in the cupboard – I thought she never knew where I was – but she did – she just sort of was happy for me to be hidden if you know what I'm saying – |

RICK    I think I do.

TALC    One time, we were round the house – and I showed
        – Fiz was the only one who I'd have in the house –
        only one I'd want in the house – and I showed her
        – and she didn't say anything – just climbed in and
        then I climbed in with her – and I didn't hate that
        cupboard so much after that.

RICK    She's a special girl.

TALC    I'm going to marry her.

RICK    Okay. Good. I think.

TALC    I need you to tell her that the playground matters.

RICK    Why would I make a difference?

TALC    You're the only one she listened to before.

RICK    I don't think – I don't think –

TALC    Because if it didn't matter – it's all we've done
        see – really – us lot – so if it didn't matter – then
        we don't matter, you understand?

        *RICK looks at TALC and then nods.*

RICK    Yes. I understand.

TALC    They're taking it down.

RICK    I know.

TALC    You got till the last thing comes down to
        persuade her.

RICK    Or what?

TALC    Or I don't like you no more.

        *Pause. RICK is slightly stunned by the simplicity
        of this.*

        You starting your new job today?

RICK    Yes.

TALC    You should go then.

RICK    Yes.

RICK *walks away. He turns and looks at* TALC
*and then he walks on.*

TALC      (*Singing*.) The muffled sounds
          I find a comfort
          The way they sit
          Outside my head

*Suddenly* FIZ *is sitting behind him.*

TALC *doesn't turn around to look at her. But he
knows she's there.*

*Beautiful noises begin underneath.*

I like the noise
Of a life outside
It makes me feel
It's okay out there

Sometimes I hear
Some things that frighten
Sometimes I hear
Some things that scare me

But then I shut my ears
And I sing this song
Then I refuse to hear
What Mum says

The muffled sounds
I find a comfort
The way they sit
Outside my head

Because that's life in the cupboard.
That's how life is – inside a cupboard.

FIZ       He likes the noise
          Of a life outside
          It makes him feel
          It's shit out there

          Sometimes he hears
          Things that frighten
          Sometimes he hears
          Things that scare him.

| | |
|---|---|
| FIZ | But then he shut his ears |
| TALC | But then I shut my ears |
| FIZ | And he sings this song |
| TALC | And I sing this song |
| FIZ | Then he refuses to hear |
| TALC | Then I refuse to hear |

FIZ *and* TALC

What his/my mum says

Because that's life in the cupboard.
That's how life is – inside a cupboard.
That's how his/my life is – in his/my cupboard.

| | |
|---|---|
| TALC | And then came you. |
| FIZ | Then came me. |
| TALC | And you opened the doors |
| FIZ | And I dragged you out. |
| TALC | And you smashed my cupboard |
| FIZ | And I smashed your cupboard |

FIZ *and* TALC

And now I'm out. Now I'm free.
The only trouble is – the we has become me.


## Scene Six

MALCOLM   Was this you?

GINGER   You seem angry, sir.

MALCOLM   I am angry. I am furious. Because frankly – this is criminal damage.

GINGER   I would say – when it comes to fury – you should be careful, sir. I heard about this guy right – he got so angry – furious – he exploded. Literally. His brain overheated. His brain literally melted out of his eyes.

MALCOLM   John –

GINGER   Ginger.

MALCOLM     Your name is John.

GINGER      No. It's Ginger.

MALCOLM     Ginger. Please don't make me expel you.

GINGER      It wasn't me.
            I wish it was.
            It wasn't me.

MALCOLM     David...

HIGGY       No one calls me David, sir.

MALCOLM     Were you responsible for this, David?

HIGGY       The Spider being built back, sir?

MALCOLM     It was The Spider?

HIGGY       Yes, sir. Overnight, sir. I mean, to do that
            overnight. That takes quite something.
            The Spider is quite a complicated framework. Sir.

MALCOLM     We're trying to demolish the playground –

HIGGY       I know.

MALCOLM     So putting up The Spider again –

HIGGY       I know. Really annoying, sir. For you, sir.

MALCOLM     I'm going to ask you a simple question, Matilda.
            Were you responsible for the criminal damage
            being done to my maths foundations...?

TILLY       You know, I never considered it like that, but
            maths do have foundations, don't they?
            Through history I guess.

MALCOLM     We'll just tear it down again.

TILLY       I know. You already tore it down twice already.
            Funny thing is, though, Mr McKendrick.
            Whenever you tear it down, someone builds it
            back up.
            Guess killing spiders is harder than you thought.

MALCOLM     I'm taking security measures...

TILLY        Good luck with that. We've found security works
             well…

MALCOLM  You will pay.

             MALCOLM *turns to the audience.*

             (*Singing.*) It's hard.
             Running a school.
             You think it'd be cool
             Running a school.
             But it's hard.
             Running a school.

             There's papers on every chair
             Papers in every drawer.
             Papers in my desk and –
             Papers in my soul.

             Because –
             It's hard
             Running a school
             You think it'd be cool.
             Running a school.
             But it's hard.
             Running a school.

             There's decisions to be made
             Decisions every day
             Decisions about yes or no –
             Decisions that decide things.

             It's hard.
             Running a school
             You think it'd be cool.
             Running a school.
             But it's hard.
             Running a school.

             Kids are shits
             This much is true
             You are a target to hit
             They try to annihilate you.

Kids are shits
And yet it's true
However much I regret it
Teaching is what I was born to do.

## Scene Seven

GINGER     Everyone knows it's you, you know…

TALC       What?

GINGER     Everyone knows it's you. The invisible person –
           putting up The Spider.

TALC       You think I'm the invisible man?

GINGER     It's what you do, isn't it?

TALC       You were going to find who did it.
           Who did it to her…
           Have you?

GINGER     No.
           The police aren't having much luck neither.
           Is it you?

TALC       No.

GINGER     But you would say that.

TALC       No. I'd probably tell you the truth.
           It's not me putting it up.
           I wish it was.

GINGER     I said that.

           *Pause.*

           And it's not Fiz.

TALC       No. It's not Fiz. She hates it.

GINGER     Do you think she's right to – hate it?

| | |
|---|---|
| TALC | No. Do you? |
| GINGER | No. |
| | *Beat.* |
| | Who gave you that nickname? Talc? |
| TALC | You. |
| GINGER | Did I? |
| TALC | It was after we had beginners swimming at Bristol North. Told me I stank. You poured talc all over my head as you did it. Said you were baptising me. |
| GINGER | Fucking hated swimming. |
| TALC | That's because you were terrible at it. You basically mostly drowned. |
| | GINGER *nods*. |
| GINGER | Talc… |
| TALC | What? |
| GINGER | My brother knows. Who did it. To her. |
| TALC | Oh. |
| GINGER | Says he'll tell me. If I want. But that if I do anything about it. People will get hurt and not just me. |
| TALC | Even if you told the police. |
| GINGER | Especially if I did that. I don't know what to do. |
| TALC | Do you trust your brother? |
| GINGER | No. |
| TALC | Do you think he's right about this? |
| GINGER | Yeah. |
| TALC | Do you think it'll change anything for the better? Getting justice – for her? |
| GINGER | I don't know. |

TALC        I don't think it will. I think it'll make things
            worse. And I think this place is about making
            things better. And I don't want it to be about
            making things worse. And I think Fiz would
            probably agree with me. If you were to tell her.
            Which I don't think you should. Because she
            doesn't need to know. And thinking about it will
            only upset her.

GINGER      You talk a lot when you talk, don't you?

TALC        Yeah.

            *There's a beat.*

GINGER      A few of us are going out tonight. Getting some
            cans in, going down the canal or the park or the
            train station maybe. Bit of a laugh. You can come
            if you like…

TALC        What?

GINGER      Do you fancy going for a beer tonight? You don't
            have to drink if you don't want to. Just hang
            about I guess.

TALC        When?

GINGER      Tonight.

TALC        Okay.

            *Pause.*

GINGER      Sorry. About the baptising.

TALC        That's okay. You weren't to know…

GINGER      Weren't to know what?

TALC        That you'd eventually like me.

            GINGER *smiles.*

GINGER      Bring cash. If you want beer. Bring cash. I'm not
            subbing you.

TALC        Right you are.

## Scene Eight

DEBBIE *leans down from an 'upstairs window' (within the playground).*

DEBBIE      She don't want to see you.

RICK        I know that, I just wanted to say –

DEBBIE      Don't matter what you wanted to say – she don't want to see you.

            *Beat.*

RICK        Can you pass on a message?

DEBBIE      As long as it's short.

RICK        Can you tell her...

            *He thinks.*

            She asked me once why I was involved in the playground in the first place. And I can't even remember what I said but I think I probably – I don't think I answered her hugely well. The truth is, I think, I think it's pretty hard being a kid. I remember – quite clearly – at the age of ten thinking it's more than possible I'd never have friends ever again. I think you think these big thoughts. Kids do think big thoughts. But I'm not sure we're tuned in to listening enough. I think mostly through my childhood I felt scared. And above all else, all I really wanted to do is create somewhere safe – create somewhere that it's okay to... But it went wrong. She wasn't safe. And I think that was my fault.

            *Pause. He almost starts to cry.*

DEBBIE      Sorry, you expect me to remember all that? Cos I ain't good at remembering.

RICK        Can you tell her sorry?

            *Pause.*

| DEBBIE | Yeah, that's dead easy to say. |
| RICK | I should have asked you to get involved, Debbie. |
| DEBBIE | Yeah, you should. I'll tell her what you said. |

## Scene Nine

| MALCOLM | They call you Loppy? Would you like to be called Loppy? |
| LOPPY | That or Keith. Either is fine. Or just anything. I actually don't mind being called anything. You could call me Anything – as in Anything – the actual word – and I probably wouldn't even mind that. I'm very easy to please. |
| | MALCOLM *hesitates*. |
| MALCOLM | Keith. |
| | I've been looking at your reports. You've been doing okay. You're clearly a bright boy. |
| LOPPY | Thank you, sir. My mother wants me to do well, sir. I try hard for my mum, sir. Is this office hot, sir? |
| MALCOLM | No. It's a regular temperature. Anyway – |
| LOPPY | Anything... |
| MALCOLM | Anyway, I hope you don't mind, but I've been talking to a few sixth forms about your abilities. There's a few that are interested in taking you in. |
| LOPPY | Okay... Um... |
| MALCOLM | You don't seem very pleased. |
| LOPPY | I'm thirteen, sir. |
| MALCOLM | I know, Keith, but with education it pays to think ahead. |

LOPPY        Okay, sir.

MALCOLM   My point is I want you to think about the future.
            And I think your mother does too.

            LOPPY *shuts his eyes.*

LOPPY        Okay, sir. She does, sir.

MALCOLM   Why have you shut your eyes?

LOPPY        I am thinking about the future. Now.

MALCOLM   No. No need to shut your eyes.
            Keith. Keith. Open your eyes.

LOPPY        Just thinking about the future, sir...
            Do you think that robots will eventually rule the
            world, sir?

MALCOLM   I'm more worried about the Russians to be
            honest, son.
            Keith. You're clearly a fine boy, with a strong
            upbringing behind him. And I need help. And
            I need it from someone who cares... about the
            future.

LOPPY        About the robots ruling the world? I care about
            that.

MALCOLM   Yes. That. Almost.
            Anyway, would you be interested in talking to
            me?
            For your future. For your mother.

            LOPPY *looks at him. He thinks. He turns.*

LOPPY        (*Singing.*) The clever bastard and my mum.
            The clever bastard and my mum.
            The clever bastard and my mum.
            The clever bastard and my mum.

**Scene Ten**

| | |
|---|---|
| GINGER | It was Rick, of course. |
| RICK | Was it? |

*They throw him a piece of wood, he starts to hammer it into the ground.*

| | |
|---|---|
| TALC | Yeah. It was. |
| GINGER | Well, the first night it was… |
| RICK | I deny everything. |
| TILLY | No you don't. |
| RICK | No, okay, I don't. |
| TALC | And then after that? |
| HIGGY | Well.<br>The second night – I got – I was curious…<br>I'd seen what had happened and – |
| RICK | He was there at 2 a.m. His jeans pulled over his pyjamas. |
| HIGGY | I don't wear pyjamas. Need to let my balls roam at night. Don't want pants during the day neither. My balls need to roam during the day too. |
| RICK | I was only going up there to look the second night. Because I couldn't sleep. Again. I'd made my protest the first night, I wasn't intending on doing it the second night.<br>But then he was there… |

*They start to build together.*

| | |
|---|---|
| HIGGY | Well, as soon as I saw him…<br>I wanted to do my bit.<br>I wanted to be part of it. |
| RICK | We worked quicker. The two of us. |
| HIGGY | But I didn't tell a soul. |
| RICK | No, you did. |

| | |
|---|---|
| HIGGY | I didn't. |
| RICK | Then how come the others turned up? |
| GINGER | We wanted to see. Someone was fucking doing it. We wanted to see who. |
| TILLY | The third night a few of us turned up. Me. Obviously. |
| GINGER | Me and Talc too. |
| TALC | Yeah. |
| TILLY | Hopeful there might be – Hopeful it might start again… |
| GINGER | I just wanted to see. |

*Now everyone starts to build.*

*And it's fast and furious but, above all, silent work.*

*And there's something flamboyant about it.*

*These* KIDS *are good builders now.*

| | |
|---|---|
| RICK | They wanted to make a few pieces. I said it had to be The Spider. Only The Spider. The Spider had symbolism. |
| HIGGY | There you go see – using wanky words again. The Spider was easy to build. |
| GINGER | They didn't know what it meant. Course. They'd tear it down – |
| TILLY | We'd build it up. Invisibly in the night. |
| TALC | Piece by piece. |
| HIGGY | It confused them. Made them slightly mental to be honest. |
| TILLY | Why The Spider? What does The Spider mean? |
| RICK | On the sixth night they had a man sitting in his car watching… |
| HIGGY | We just waited for him to sleep. |

| | |
|---|---|
| GINGER | And he fell asleep with his window open. Summer balmy night, course he did. |
| TILLY | So we reached in and lifted his handbrake. |
| HIGGY | And we pushed him for forty-five minutes into the centre of the St Paul's estate. |
| GINGER | He must have shit himself when he woke up in the morning. |
| TILLY | You don't want to wake up in St Paul's. |
| RICK | It was quite fun. |
| TILLY | The seventh night the guy fell asleep with his window closed. |
| GINGER | So we painted his windscreen white. |
| HIGGY | And then... |
| GINGER | And then... |
| TILLY | And then... |
| LOPPY | The eighth night. I came. |

*They stop building.*

And they didn't know to hide from me.
And I didn't know...
Well, I did know.
I told the head for my mum.
And the robots.

| | |
|---|---|
| HIGGY | And once they knew – once Loppy told them – the fizz went bang. You know? |
| TILLY | The fizz went what? |
| HIGGY | As soon as they knew – their own teacher – one of their own – a man they paid – |
| GINGER | Rick. |
| RICK | Me. |
| HIGGY | As soon as they knew he was behind it – I mean, us, they'd have got pissed off with – |

| | |
|---|---|
| GINGER | A couple of months of detentions for Higgy, Talc and Tilly. An expulsion for me. |
| HIGGY | But Rick – |
| TALC | Rick doing it – really pissed them off. |
| TILLY | Really pissed them off. |
| HIGGY | And so they called the police. |
| TILLY | They did, you know?<br>They called the law. |
| GINGER | And that's where I stepped in – because, you see I've got a police radio… |
| RICK | What? |
| GINGER | A police radio. |
| RICK | You've got a police radio? |
| GINGER | It's my brother's. But he sort of – I listen for him. I report in. |
| RICK | Okay. That's not… |
| GINGER | And so when they called the police – I called everyone…<br>Meet at the playground. |
| RICK | Meet where? |
| HIGGY | Where else? The playground. |
| RICK | Shouldn't we just – meet at someone's house or… |
| GINGER | No. We're meeting at the playground. |
| TILLY | I don't really like calling it a playground. |
| HIGGY | They called the police. |
| GINGER | We called each other. |
| HIGGY | We got him up the playground. |
| TILLY | And we got ready – ready to protect him. |

## Scene Eleven

*The music is frantic.*

GINGER      (*Singing.*) When I was a kid I liked nothing.
            I'd do nothing most of the day.
            When I was a kid I liked nothing.
            I'd fill entire days with shit.

            *The junk gets rearranged into a sort of barrier.*

            *Think* Les Misérables. *But perhaps slightly less
            extensive. And, you know, French.*

EVERYONE    We'll fight for The Spider, fight for the ship
            Fight for the thing where we do dip-the-dip
            We haven't quite worked out why it's the biz
            But we'll fight for whatever it is.

TILLY       When I was a kid I was mostly afraid.
            I could be afraid of virtually anything.
            I'd hide under the covers
            And shiver and wish I was a ghost.

EVERYONE    We'll fight for The Spider, fight for the ship
            Fight for the thing where we do dip-the-dip
            We haven't quite worked out why it's the biz
            But we'll fight for whatever it is.

            RICK *stands ready to sing a verse. He opens his
            mouth, but he's unbearably moved.*

RICK        (*Tries to sing.*) When I –
            (*Singing.*) I am so –
            (*Spoken.*) You guys are the best.

GINGER      We protect our own.

            HIGGY *and* GINGER *walk along the ramparts.*

HIGGY       Fuck me.

GINGER      That's actually – quite cool.

HIGGY       Yeah.

            TALC *sticks his head up.*

TALC        How better to protect him than with junk.

> *They hum as the noise of a siren permeates the air.*

GINGER     They went to his house first. Course.

POLICE     Rick. Rick. Don't make a mess of this. Rick.

EVERYONE   (*Singing.*) Rick. Rick. Don't make a mess of this. Rick.

HIGGY      Then they went to his girlfriend's house.

POLICE     We're just interested in talking to Rick. Is he here?

EVERYONE   (*Singing.*) Rick. Rick. Don't make a mess of this. Rick.

TILLY      Never knew you had a girlfriend, Rick.

RICK       Alice. She's called. She's recent.

EVERYONE   (*Singing.*) Rick. Rick. Don't make a mess of this. Rick.

HIGGY      And then they came here.

HIGGY      They shouted up – just –

POLICE     (*Singing.*) Rick.

EVERYONE   Rick.

POLICE     (*Singing.*) Rick.

EVERYONE   Rick.

POLICE     (*Singing.*) Rick.

EVERYONE   (*Singing.*) Rick. Rick. Don't make a mess of this. Rick.

TALC       And then the headmaster arrived.

EVERYONE   (*Singing.*) Rick. Rick. Don't make a mess of this. Rick.

MALCOLM    Okay. This is just silly.
           Can everyone please – can everyone please stop –

GINGER     Silly?

TILLY        You're the one who called the police.

MALCOLM   I just want to talk to my colleague.

HIGGY       You normally bring police when you come and
            talk to your colleague? You're here to take Rick
            away. And then you'll take the playground away.

MALCOLM   The playground is coming down...

TILLY        Listen to yourself, that sounds silly too.

MALCOLM   And you are all going to –
            You are all going to have to –
            Learn how to – behave.

TILLY        And that sounds really silly.

MALCOLM   You will learn how to behave and...

GINGER     But we don't want to. Behave. Not on this.

MALCOLM   Ginger –

TILLY        We don't though, sir. We really don't. We like
            it here.

GINGER     Loppy. We forgive you. Just so you know.

LOPPY      What? Yeah? How did you know it was me?

HIGGY       You weren't subtle, son. You kept writing things
            down.

LOPPY      I was just doing it for the future – the robots and
            stuff.

TILLY        We forgive you. But we're not going to behave.

GINGER     We don't have it in us.

MALCOLM   But – but –

GINGER     But what?

MALCOLM   But get down from there otherwise we'll have to
            come arrest you. All. You can ruin all your
            futures here.

GINGER     I've never believed in the future.

RICK            Maybe he's right.

EVERYONE (*Singing.*) Rick. Rick. Don't make a mess of this.
                Rick.

MALCOLM    Rick. Please. Do the decent thing here.

EVERYONE (*Singing.*) Rick. Rick. Don't make a mess of this.
                Rick.

RICK            I'm not having you risking your futures.

HIGGY          We don't care about the future.

TILLY           We care about this, now. And we care about you.
                You understood nothing?

RICK            And I care about you. And that means going with
                them. Malcolm. I'm coming.

MUM            No. You're not.

                *And now the junk falls away as* FIZ's MUM
                *comes triumphantly up the stage towards us.*

HIGGY          Who called her?

                DEBBIE *appears behind her* MUM.

DEBBIE        Ginger called me. He told me loved me. He told
                me to go get my mum.

HIGGY          Ginger told you he loved you?

DEBBIE        Doesn't even care if the kid is yours.

HIGGY          Don't you?

GINGER        Least he won't be ginger.

MUM            I thought I'd say my piece.
                I'm here to say my piece.
                Headmaster. Malcolm. Can I call you Malcolm?

MALCOLM    I don't think that's appropriate in front of the kids.

MUM            This place – hurt my daughter. But it also was
                somewhere she loved. She got hurt fighting for it.
                But she'd never fought for nowhere before.

MALCOLM    I understand that but...

| | |
|---|---|
| MUM | Well, isn't that good?<br>Good for them to do something they love? Good<br>for them to have somewhere… |
| MALCOLM | Not if it's dangerous. Not if it damages them.<br>Rick. Get down. |
| RICK | I'm coming. I'm coming.<br>(*Turns to the* KIDS.) We're done. We tried. You<br>tried. Thank you for coming. |
| FIZ | (*From offstage*.) No. No. No.<br>For fuck's sake, I was trying to stay out of this.<br>Can you people really do nothing without me? |

*She wheels herself on in a wheelchair.*

| | |
|---|---|
| TALC | Fiz. You're here? |
| FIZ | Yeah yeah 'Fiz's here'. Mum, I told you to do<br>this without me. |
| MUM | I tried. |
| FIZ | You failed. And talking of failures, sir, you come<br>down one more plank and I'll plank you. |
| RICK | This was my fault. |
| FIZ | Can we stop that? Can we stop it being his fault,<br>your fault, my fault. This is our playground, isn't<br>it? It's all our fault. |
| TALC | Our playground. |
| FIZ | Listen, talky, you got well out of hand since I've<br>been ill, making friends even, congratulations on<br>that, but enough with the heckling okay? |
| TALC | Understood. |
| FIZ | Right. Now I better say something important<br>better I? Cos you're all listening. Well… The<br>thing I got to say is…<br>(*Licks her lips, she composes herself.*)<br>Mr McKendrick. You're better than this. |
| MALCOLM | I don't think throwing insults – |

FIZ             (*Interrupting.*) But we're not. You go off – run
                your school – but this bit – if you don't mind –
                leave this bit for us. Because this bit. It matters.
                To us. And school – it just doesn't. You know it.
                I know it.

MALCOLM   You were hurt.

FIZ             Yup. Things get hurt though don't they?

MALCOLM   You were unsupervised.

FIZ             I was alone because I chose to be alone because
                I can be a silly bitch sometimes. In fact, a very
                silly bitch. But the thing is, I was a lonely silly
                bitch, and then you gave us this place. Then you
                gave us Rick. Then you gave us each other.
                Thanks for your message, Rick, unnecessary, but
                appreciated.

RICK           My – pleasure.

FIZ             Look, Mr McKendrick, I thought it meant
                nothing – the playground – but then I kept
                thinking – about it – and if you keep thinking
                about something – it can't mean nothing can it?

                (*Singing.*) The best of us.
                In here, is the best of us.
                Look at it, it's nuts and brilliant.
                As nuts and brilliant as we think we are.

                The best of us.
                In here, is the best of us.
                It's broken, it's shit, it doesn't fit.
                As broken and shit as we know we are.

                The best of us.
                In here, is the best of us.
                A cupboard for us to be made anew.
                A cupboard for us to work out what we are.

                It's a plastercast.
                It's the plastercast we need.
                It's the plastercast that will feed
                Us as we grow old here.

I mean, look at it. Maths won't teach us fuck-all,
but this place, this place…

This is a Spider, this is a ship
This is the thing where we do dip-the-dip
We haven't quite worked out what this thing is
But we promise you it is the biz.

*She looks around.*

I'd really expect someone to have joined in by
now.
Fine.
I sat on one of them machines.
I sat there thinking I was dying.
And the one thing that made me smile.
And I really didn't want it to.
Was this place.
Plastercast.
Talcum powder, you're with me…

FIZ *and* TALC

This is a Spider, this is a ship.

*More join in.*

This is the thing where we do dip-the-dip
We haven't quite worked out what this thing is
But we promise you it is the biz.

FIZ         (*Spoken.*) Come on, sir, if you aren't going to put
            us here where are you gonna put us?

GINGER      And don't say fucking maths.

MALCOLM     You realise it isn't entirely my decision, there are
            funding applications and…

HIGGY       But will you try, sir? That's all we want you to do
            – try.

TILLY       And sir to stay out of jail.

MALCOLM     As long as you understand I can't promise
            anything.

            *The* KIDS *cheer.*

No, no, that's a massive overreaction to a very
limited guarantee.

DEBBIE          (*Singing*.) James – a massive potato
He looked – like a massive potato
I kissed him – because I wanted him to be –
grateful.
He was nice.
Plastercast.

EVERYONE This is a Spider, this is a ship.
This is the thing where we do dip-the-dip
We haven't quite worked out what this thing is
But we promise you it is the biz.

MUM             Neil was a boring man.
He'd want news followed by news.
He'd want lager followed by lager.
He'd scream and he'd shout about what
was wrong.
And then fix none of it.
Plastercast.

MALCOLM It's hard.
Running a school.
You think it'd be cool
Running a school.
But it's hard.
Running a school.
Plastercast.

EVERYONE This is a Spider, this is a ship.
This is the thing where we do dip-the-dip
We haven't quite worked out what this thing is
But we promise you it is the biz.

TALC            Sometimes I hear
Things that frighten
Sometimes I hear
Things that scare me
But then I shut my ears
And I sing this song
Then I refuse to hear

                    What Mum says
                    Plastercast.

GINGER          I remember very clearly
                    My first visit to a pub
                    My brother was all cheery
                    We even had some grub
                    But then it went
                    A little bit wrong
                    But then it got
                    A little too strong
                    Cos fighting is how you belong.

GINGER *and* HIGGY
                    He beat a man black and blue
                    He could have killed him if he wanted to
                    He looked at me like I should have been proud
                    I was not.
                    Plastercast.

EVERYONE    The best of us.
                    In here, is the best of us.
                    Look at it, it's nuts and brilliant.
                    As nuts and brilliant as we think we are.

                    The best of us.
                    In here, is the best of us.
                    It's broken, it's shit, it doesn't fit.
                    As broken and shit as we know we are.

                    The best of us.
                    In here, is the best of us.
                    A cupboard for us to be made anew.
                    A cupboard for us to work out what we are.

                    It's a plastercast.
                    It's the plastercast we need.
                    It's the plastercast that will feed
                    Us as we grow old here.

RICK            (*Alone*.) This is a Spider, this is a ship.
                    This is the thing where we do dip-the-dip
                    We haven't quite worked out what this thing is
                    But we promise you it is the biz.

*The audience are encouraged to applaud.*

*The cast take their bows.*

*As they do the medley gets more raucous.*

*And in the middle of it,* FIZ *stands up and walks to the front.*

FIZ          I bet you thought you'd find out who did it to me.
             Ginger the Great Mouse Detective never even
             told me so he's hardly going to tell you.
             Just to be clear.
             I was assaulted and left for dead – by someone –
             and that person – was never caught.
             He's probably sitting beside you right now.
             Yeah. That guy. No – on the other side.
             And I bet you thought she'd give birth to that
             baby at some big moment.
             Which she actually did do.
             But that had nothing to do with the playground.
             In fact, that's another story entirely.
             Anyway…
             Lockleaze Playground in Romney Avenue,
             Bristol, has been open now for over forty years.
             There are hundreds like it all over the country.
             Every year they threaten it with closure. Every
             year the hours it stays open get less and less.
             Because of cuts and the fact that kids have been
             abusing it.
             Kids will always abuse it. That's why it's there.
             That's the point.
             And money should be spent on it.
             Because our faces change – and the things we do
             change – but need, need never changes.
             We're old now, some of us are older than you
             now, but what this did for us, that's still there.

TILLY        I'm a bookmaker. I specialise in taking bets on
             the length of celebrity marriages.

HIGGY        I'm in jail. Credit-card fraud. But they haven't
             found where I've stashed the money.

TALC        I'm one of the most popular vloggers on
            YouTube. Particularly amongst Chilean
            housewives. They like me with my top off.

FIZ         Do they?

TALC        Okay, I'm an electrical engineer. For BT. I install
            your wireless mainly.

LOPPY       I can hear. Cochlear implants. I don't like it.
            I work in sewage.

GINGER      And I'm a priest. No, really I am. I know.
            Surprised me too.

FIZ         And me? I'm actually, as it turns out, a teacher.
            Not a good one, turns out I sometimes hit
            children, but, you know, I teach. Or try to. Rick's
            my boss actually. A headmaster now. And you
            know, he tries – to make me stop hitting children.
            And occasionally succeeds.
            This place made us. For good and for bad. I live
            down the street from my mum and my sister
            Debbie. Who has now had five children.

DEBBIE      They're a nightmare.

FIZ         And I still know most of the guys. In fact, when
            Talc and Tilly got married, it was Ginger who
            did the service. Very good job he did too. His
            sermon was quite moving. No, none of us
            understand it either.
            My point is…
            We sort of stayed stuck together. Because that's
            the way we were made.
            This is our place.
            It made us.
            And I think we needed it – need it.
            We've been junk. You've been lovely. Thanks for
            coming to see us play.

# Headlong

Headlong: /hedl'ong/ noun 1. with head first, 2. starting boldly, 3. to approach with speed and vigour

**Headlong** creates exhilarating contemporary theatre: a provocative mix of innovative new writing, reimagined classics and influential twentieth century plays that illuminate our world. Touring exceptional theatre around the UK lies at the heart of what we do; we also present work on major London stages and internationally. We encourage the best emerging artists and more established talent to create their most exciting work with us. We place digital innovation at the forefront of all our activities - building inventive online content to sit alongside our productions to enrich audiences' understanding of our work.

Our productions have included *This House* (Chichester Festival Theatre and West End), *Pygmalion* (UK tour), *Boys Will Be Boys* (Bush Theatre), *People, Places and Things* (National Theatre and West End), *1984* (UK and international tour and West End), *The Nether* (Royal Court and West End), *American Psycho* (Almeida and Broadway), *Chimerica* (Almeida and West End), and *Enron* (UK tour, West End and Broadway).

In 2017 Jeremy Herrin will direct Anne-Marie Duff in D.C. Moore's new play *Common* at the National Theatre; *1984* returns for an extensive Australian tour and concurrently opens on Broadway; *People, Places and Things* tours the UK with a brand new cast, whilst Denise Gough reprises her role along with the original cast for a run at St. Ann's Warehouse, New York this autumn.

West End cast for *People, Places and Things*, 2016 Photo: Johan Persson

# Headlong Staff

**Artistic Director**
Jeremy Herrin
**Executive Director**
Alan Stacey
**Finance Manager**
Julie Renwick
**Administrative Producer**
Fran du Pille
**Associate Producer**
Liz Eddy
**Associate General Manager**
Amy Michaels
**Assistant Producer**
Alecia Marshall

**Development Manager**
Joshua Chua
**Marketing Officer**
Olivia Farrant
**Administrator**
Ellie Claughton
**Creative Associate**
Amy Hodge
**Production Manager**
Simon Evans
**Press Agent**
Clióna Roberts
**Fundraising Consultant**
Kirstin Peltonen
**Outreach Associate**
Rob Watt

*'Slams down with that characteristic Headlong rush'*
The Observer
on *People, Places and Things*.

*'The indefatigably inventive Headlong'*
The Times on *1984*

Visit our website
**www.headlong.co.uk**
for news of forthcoming projects,
to join our mailing list, and to find out
how you can support our work.

Follow @HeadlongTheatre on Twitter.

Supported using public funding by
**ARTS COUNCIL ENGLAND**

# Bristol Old Vic

## Creating the future, inspired by the past.

**Bristol Old Vic is the oldest continuously-working theatre in the United Kingdom. Our mission is to create pioneering 21st Century theatre in partnership with the people of Bristol; inspired by the history and magical design of the most beautiful playhouse in the country.**

We are led by artists who see the world with distinctive clarity and whose ability to articulate what they see allows us to understand and engage with our world afresh. Our programme includes original productions, artist development and outreach work that connects on a local, national and international level.

In 2016, Bristol Old Vic marked our 250th birthday, celebrating with a season of work from the theatre's history as well as our future. Work also began on the final phase of our building's capital development, which will deliver a new foyer and studio theatre in 2018 designed by Stirling Prize winning architects Haworth Tompkins.

**0117 987 7877
bristololdvic.org.uk**

King St, Bristol BS1 4ED
🐦 📘 @BristolOldVic

Supported by
**ARTS COUNCIL
ENGLAND**

Charity No. 228235

Supported by
**The National Lottery®**
through the Heritage Lottery Fund

heritage
lottery fund

# ROSE THEATRE KINGSTON

**Founded by Sir Peter Hall, and modelled on the original Elizabethan Rose Theatre on London's Bankside, Rose Theatre Kingston is the largest producing theatre in South West London.**

Since opening in 2008, the Rose has collaborated with a range of directors, playwrights and producing partners to create vibrant, engaging and inspiring productions. Following on the success of *The Wars of the Roses* trilogy directed by Trevor Nunn, this year the Rose will be presenting another theatrical event and world première – Elena Ferrante's celebrated quartet of novels *My Brilliant Friend*. The two-part adaptation of Ferrante's gripping family saga is brought to the stage for the first time by director Melly Still, starring Niamh Cusack and Catherine McCormack.

Recent works include Zach Helm's *Good Canary* directed by John Malkovich, David Hare's *The Absence of War* directed by Jeremy Herrin, Alan Bennett's *Single Spies* directed by Sarah Esdaile, Jacqueline Wilson's *Hetty Feather* (West End transfer and Olivier Award nominee) directed by Sally Cookson and Brian Friel's *Translations* (Winner of the UK Theatre Award for Best Touring Production) directed by James Grieve.

Photos by Mark Douet:(from top to bottom) *Good Canary, All My Sons, The Wind in the Willows*

**Chief Executive** Robert O'Dowd
**Executive Producer** Jerry Gunn

# rosetheatrekingston.org

*World class theatre on your doorstep*

# Theatr Clwyd

---

**'One of the hidden treasures of North Wales, a huge vibrant culture complex'**

*Guardian*

Theatr Clwyd is one of the foremost producing theatres in Wales – a beacon of excellence looking across the Clwydian Hills yet only forty minutes from Liverpool.

Since 1976 we have been a theatrical powerhouse and much-loved home for our community. Now, led by the new Executive team of Tamara Harvey and Liam Evans-Ford, we are going from strength to strength producing world-class theatre, from new plays to classic revivals.

We have three theatres, a cinema, café, bar and art galleries and, alongside our own shows, offer a rich and varied programme of visual arts, film, theatre, music, dance and comedy. We also work extensively with our local community, schools and colleges and create award-winning work for, with and by young people. In our fortieth year we will have co-produced with the Wales Millennium Centre, Sherman Theatre, Gagglebabble and The Other Room in Cardiff, Paines Plough, Vicky Graham Productions at the Yard Theatre, High Tide, Hampstead Theatre, Bristol Old Vic, The Rose Theatre, Kingston, Headlong and Sheffield Theatres.

Over 200,000 people a year come through our doors and in 2015 Theatr Clwyd was voted the Most Welcoming Theatre in Wales.

**'Absolute must-see productions'** *Western Mail*

**01352 701521**
**www.theatrclwyd.com**

*Cat on a Hot Tin Roof.* Photo: Johan Persson